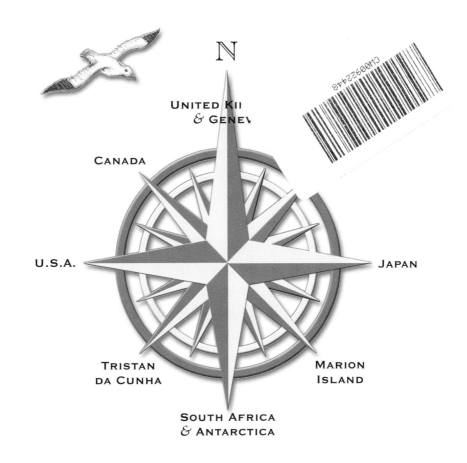

N

UNITED KII
& GENE\

CANADA

U.S.A.

JAPAN

TRISTAN
DA CUNHA

MARION
ISLAND

SOUTH AFRICA
& ANTARCTICA

Memoirs:
North, South, East & West

ALLAN B. CRAWFORD M.B.E.

GEORGE MANN PUBLICATIONS

Published by
George Mann Publications
Easton, Winchester,
Hampshire SO21 1ES
01962 779944

A CIP catalogue record for this book
is available from the British Library

ISBN 0954629981

Other titles by this author:

I went to Tristan
(Hodder & Stoughton 1941)

The Tristan Times
(published as a limited edition, 1943)

Tristan da Cunha and the Roaring Forties
(Charles Skilton / David Philip 1982, 0284985899)

Penguins, Potatoes and Postage Stamps
(Anthony Nelson, 1999, 0904614689)

Tristan da Cunha: Wartime Invasion
(George Mann Publications, 2004, 0954629914)

George Mann Publications

Dedication

It is for me a great pleasure and privilege as an ex-naval reserve officer and maritime meteorologist to dedicate these memoirs to my favourite charity.

On hearing of this idea, Mrs Judy Polkinhorn, Executive Director of Mercy Ships, expressed her wholehearted support.

I cannot find better words than to quote briefly what Lord Carey, former Archbishop of Canterbury, contributed to their brochure:

> '*I am very pleased to be associated with this Christian Charity which provides care and healing free of charge to the poorest and neediest people in the world. The dedication and the love of the self-supporting volunteers on board the ships is an inspiration to us all.*'

Anyone interested in serving or donating towards this international fleet of ships should contact: Mercy Ships UK, The Lighthouse, 12 Meadway Court, Stevenage SG1 2EF, UK ~ telephone: 01438 727800 ~ email: info@mercyships.org.uk.

What do you think? Bathsheba, my cat, providing editorial assistance (*photo: Sally McKenzie*)

Preface

During the year 2006 Tristan da Cunha celebrates the Quincentenary of its discovery by the Portuguese Admiral of that name who placed it on the charts. Several ceremonies, including a cruise to the islands were planned both in the islands and in the United Kingdom throughout 2006 in which, due to my age, sadly, I cannot easily take part directly.

I have, however, taken indirect part by producing these memoirs which start in 1911, the year before my birth, and have been completed in my 95th year. Hopefully all the facts and dates quoted in the following pages are accurate.

On 12 September 2006, age 94, I completed the proofreading of the final paragraph of this book. A bottle of champagne, presented especially for the occasion by Professor Hans and Mrs Rausing of Wadhurst Park, was opened to celebrate the day.

Allan Crawford

Acknowledgements

To write these justifiably for a lifetime of 90 years I find is almost an impossibility, but one has to make a start; I find it easier to work backwards – starting from today.

Friend George Mann of Easton, Winchester whom I am lucky enough to have for advice on the production of my memoirs, comes first on my list. I then think of my home-help, Tina, who is already mentioned in the text. She is followed by Sally McKenzie as a superb photographer, Karen Marr my typist of Flimwell and Liz Evans my dentist of Tunbridge Wells who likewise are mentioned elsewhere in the book.

I have good friends in the Tristan da Cunha Association like Ron Burn, Lorna Smith, Guy and Elizabeth Marriott and many more, as well as Tristan islanders who are still alive whom I met in 1937 when I first visited the island.

My younger son, Jamie, lives with me in my home in Wadhurst and is a great help and the local Wealden District Council kindly altered my home to enable me to stay here as long as it is possible to do so. My friends and relatives in England comprise mainly people like Miriam and Betty, the local clergy and parishioners who live in this area, and members of the retired men's club Probus who organize periodically special lunches and dinners.

I also valued greatly the help I had in the late 1980's from the Falkland Islands Association on wise procedures to adopt in forming a similar Association for Tristan da Cunha. This was followed by backing from the then Colonial Office of the day, who gave us their support. Likewise we had support from Trevor Hearl and Owen George of their respective St Helena organisations, thus keeping all informed and in the picture regarding the affairs of the British Islands in the South Atlantic Ocean.

I still think back on family and friends in South Africa like my old shipmates in the Naval Reserve, the Weather Bureau and families like the late John Marsh (my Best Man), the Moodies, Pettits and Gregorowskis to whom I owe so much.

Please accept otherwise my shortcomings.

Contents

Illustrations

Foreword

The Adminstrator
Tristan da Cunha
South Atlantic Ocean
TDCU 1ZZ

Allan Crawford's accounts of his lifelong involvement with Tristan are required reading for Administrators-designate. When preparing to take up my own posting here, I was delighted to receive an advance copy for the Island Library of his *Tristan da Cunha – Wartime Invasion* about life here in the 1940s. I was even more delighted to find this reference in a lexicon of Tristan dialect:

'*Crawford – Curious, inquisitive person ("You's an old Crawford")* *

We may safely conclude that Allan's lifelong curiosity has enabled him to compile sufficient raw material for these memoirs, produced in his 93rd year. Thank you Allan for your curiosity, for your memories, and for being such a good friend of Tristan da Cunha.

mike Hertley

January 2006

* *Daniel Schreier & Karen Lavarello-Schreier, 'Tristan da Cunha History-People-Language', Battlebridge Publications, 2003.*

(photo: Ann-Marie 1999)

Memoirs: Why?

It has been suggested I write my memoirs before I forget them. Why, I wonder should I contemplate the proposition after having written four books already about Tristan da Cunha, one of the smallest communities in the world? The main reason, I am informed, is because it is important to record certain events connected with the 40 to 50 years which are not covered in the books.

To me, my life has been like a jigsaw puzzle; all activities of the past fitting together like magic which I had only observed in my 90's, upon reflection. As I looked back some significant milestones became apparent.

~~~

The first milestone was undoubtedly the day at the end of November 1937 while travelling in the Royal Mail ship *Arundel Castle* from England to South Africa in search of a job. I did not realise it at the time but a chance meeting with fellow passenger, Dr Erling Christophersen of Oslo, was to predestine almost the whole of my future life up to my ninetieth birthday and subsequent award of the M.B.E. by Her Majesty the Queen at Buckingham Palace for my work on and for Tristan da Cunha.

~~~

The second memorable milestone was on the 28 March 1938 when *H.M.S. Milford* arrived at Tristan unexpectedly on the day before the arrival of the whale factory ship *Thorshammer* which was my only known way to return to South Africa. The *Milford's* captain, Captain R. L. B. Cunliffe R.N., graciously agreed to give me a lift direct to the Cape. By granting me passage in his ship, I was able to witness the very unusual ceremony on the following day when we sailed to the uninhabited Gough Island, 230 sea miles south of Tristan, to declare it as a British Dependency and to plant the Union Jack there as proof of British ownership!

~~~

The third milestone, metaphorically speaking, was when the Royal Navy took me under their wing when they realised I had information useful to them by having surveyed British Territory previously only sketched from the sea. No one at that time realised how useful this chart would be to the Allied Cause when hostilities broke out in 1939 and the island was developed in 1942 as a naval communication shore-base of strategic importance.

The fourth milestone was reached early in 1939, when I joined the Royal Geographical Society in London and met Antarctic pundit Dr Brian Roberts who spent half his time working at the Foreign Office in London and the rest of the week at the Scott Polar Research Institute in Cambridge. He was interested in my work in the Southern Hemisphere especially in Tristan and Gough Islands and later on Marion Island in the Indian Ocean. He asked me to consider donating my archives to the Institute, as they would be valuable for research on my demise! This I did in 1995 while I was still capable of listing them into a chronological collection in eleven box files. At that time I never imagined I would live at least another 10 years!

~~~~

My fifth milestone could be said to be the part I played in connection with the return of the Tristan islanders to their homes after the 1961 volcano eruption. They had, very wisely, been evacuated to Britain for their safety while the volcano erupted, close to the village of Edinburgh. Although the Islanders' were well-treated and cared for by the British Government, there was a hint of an intention to integrate them into UK civilisation and prevent their return to Tristan. Many Tristan families sought my help and I made representations on their behalf in support of their return to their homeland. They were eventually successful and returned to the island which they had occupied since 1816 – nearly 190 years.

~~~~

My sixth milestone was on 15 April 1987 when, on retirement in England and with the indispensable aid of Mr Michael Swales, a member of the Gough Island Scientific Survey Expedition in 1955, we formed the Tristan da Cunha Association in the U.K. at the Royal Geographical Society in London. The Association's sole interest was the welfare of the Islanders and its committee of experts and its members have helped the Islanders in many different ways, educationally and materially, especially after a devastating storm in 2001.

~~~~

Milestone number seven, I am proud to record, took place on 31 December 2001 when my name was included in the New Year's Honours List for the award of the M.B.E. for my work on behalf of the community of Tristan da Cunha. In presenting the award to me at Buckingham Palace on 19 March 2002, H.M. Queen Elizabeth expressed great interest in the welfare of the Islanders, an interest that has been maintained in the Royal Family since Queen Victoria's days.

~~~~

Many of my adventures, experiences and pieces of my life's magical jigsaw puzzle have been recorded in detail in my earlier books.

My first book, *I Went to Tristan*, was published in 1941 by Hodder and Stoughton. It was mainly about my adventures making the first proper survey of the island at the end of 1937 during a four month period when I was the surveyor with a Norwegian Scientific Expedition. It was written during the beginning of World War II at a time when stocks of printing paper were decimated by Nazi bombing on London. I have no idea how many copies were printed if indeed I ever knew.

It was to be over 40 years before my next book was published. I realised when I went on pension in 1976 that there were very few authentic books that had been published about the island; and so when my wife and I returned to Britain, I carried out research in museums and institutions in the UK and produced my second book, *Tristan da Cunha and the Roaring Forties*, published by Charles Skilton of Edinburgh in 1982. I believe over 2000 copies were printed but the firm and stocks of books no longer exist though occasionally a copy is available on a specialised or second-hand book market.

On my retirement in 1976 I took an interest in research and assisted the Crown Agents in designs for postage stamps for Tristan. My third book, *Penguins, Potatoes and Postage Stamps,* was the culmination of this work and this well-illustrated book was printed by Anthony Nelson Publishers of Oswestry in 1999. 700 copies were produced and some are still available at my home in Wadhurst, East Sussex.

My fourth book, *Tristan da Cunha: Wartime Invasion*, published in 2004 by George Mann Publications, recorded my wartime activities in South Africa and on Tristan da Cunha in 1942. During my eighteen month posting as a meteorologist I was able to undertake a unique study of the life, times and heritage of the inhabitants of the Islanders which I was able to document in words and on film.

~~~

I hope that this memoir serves up the missing pieces of the jigsaw puzzle to complete the picture.

Allan Crawford

Wadhurst, January 2006

Memoir Milestones

1912	Born 1st August, Conwy, North Wales. (British).
1922-27	Craig Preparatory School, Windermere.
1927-30	Wellington School, Somerset.
1931-36	Engineering apprentice, Vickers-Armstrongs, Barrow. (Higher National Certificate in Mechanical Engineering).
1937-38	Member of Norwegian Scientific Expedition to Tristan da Cunha as surveyor. (Admiralty Chart No. 1769 is still my survey).
1940	Joined Royal Geographical Society.
1941	Wrote book *I Went to Tristan* (Foreword by Admiral Sir E. R. G. R. Evans), published by Hodder & Stoughton
1942-43	War service on Tristan da Cunha in charge of weather station for the Royal Navy.
1941-45	War service in South African Air Force as meteorologist.
1946	Awarded B.E.M. (Military Division for War Service).
1948	In charge of weather station, Marion Island, Indian Ocean.
1949	Married Joyce Burch, broadcaster and lecturer (2 sons).
1949	Awarded Cuthbert Peak Grant, Royal Geographical Society.
1950	Served as Port Meteorological Officer, Cape Town Docks; post recommended by World Meteorological Organization (Geneva).
1952	Joined R.N.V.R. (South Africa Division) as meteorologist. Eventual rank on retirement Lieutenant-Commander.
1954-72	Attended international conferences as maritime meteorologist in U.K., Geneva, Holland, Germany, Japan and U.S.A.
1955	Appointed Honorary Welfare Officer for Tristan da Cunha in Cape Town by UK Colonial Secretary Mr. Lennox-Boyd.
1960	Invented Sea-surface Temperature Bucket , promoted by World Meteorological Organizations.
1961	Visited Bouvet Island and Antarctica on meteorological matters.
1961-63	Initiated repatriation of Tristan da Cunha islanders on their request, after volcanic eruption on the island (1961).

1963	Awarded Order of Simon of Cyrene by Archbishop of Cape Town for services to Tristan islanders.
1976	Went on pension. Returned to U.K. (Wadhurst, East Sussex).
1980	Visualized importance to U.K. of British Islands in the South Atlantic Ocean; joined Falkland Islands Association, St. Helena Link Committee and Friends of St. Helena Society.
1980-91	Eleven years Churchwarden, Tidebrook Church in Wadhurst, East Sussex.
1982	Wrote book *Tristan da Cunha: The Roaring Forties*. Foreword by H.R.H. The Duke of Edinburgh. Published by Charles Skilton Ltd.
1984	Visited Tristan da Cunha for seventh time, this time with son, Martin, and grandaughter, Shirley.
1984 onwards	Designed ten sets of commemorative postage stamps for Tristan da Cunha including: special issue for the Royal Geographical Society's 150th Anniversary; Flags; Shipwrecks (3 series); The lost lifeboat centenary; Flightlessness; etc.; including four photographs to celebrate the end of World War II (50th Anniversary) which appeared on 19 June, 1995.
1987	Formed the Tristan da Cunha Association (U.K.). First Chairman, and Editor of the Tristan da Cunha Newsletter for the first 16 editions.
1992	Retired as Chairman, and appointed the Association's first President.
1995	Presented (upon request) 11 box files of my life's archives to the Scott Polar Research Institute, Cambridge University for posterity.
1999	Published book *Penguins, Potatoes, & Postage Stamps*. Anthony Nelson Publishers.
2001	31 December: Awarded M.B.E. in New Year's Honours List. H.M.
2002	19 March: Received M.B.E. from H.M. The Queen.
2003	Made Life-President of the Tristan da Cunha Association (U.K.)
2004	Published book Tristan da Cunha: Wartime Invasion. George Mann Publications, Winchester.
2006	Quincentenary of discovery of Tristan da Cunha
2006	Donations to National Oceanography Centre, Southampton.
2006	Published Memoirs: North, South, East & West.

Jolly Jack Tar

I was born on the 1 August 1912 in the home of my maternal grandparents in a house called *Gwynfryn* (*Sunnybank*) in the district of Llanrhos, Conwy within sight of the famous castle in North Wales. My grandparents later moved to Deganwy at the mouth of the Conwy River, where my three sisters and I spent many a holiday in our later lives.

My mother was born in Lymm, Cheshire in a house called *The Chestnuts* probably in the year 1892 for she was 20 when I was born. I visited her old house in later life and it had been turned into a home for the disabled but became redundant as the result of subsequent local by-laws. Mother was typically English in origin.

My father, on the other hand, as my name implies, was of Scottish descent, but was born in the district of East Plumstead, Woolwich, Kent on the 12 October 1879. Our forefathers' graves are in the churchyard of Dunfermline Abbey, on the north bank of the Firth of Forth, Scotland. Grandfather was an engineer and married a lady called Louisa Mary Arber, of Huguenot descent, and emigrated to Woolwich and worked at the famous Arsenal. It was there that my father was educated; he also inherited his father's engineering skills.

In view of these facts, I have never known whether to consider myself to be Welsh, English or a Scot, but at least I can qualify as being unquestionably of British nationality.

For reasons of economy we lived in a seaside village called Rampside, three miles from Barrow-in-Furness, Cumbria.

~~~

My first introduction to naval affairs could be said (with a stretch of the imagination) to have started in 1917 at the age of 5 towards the end of the Great War. I had by then 3 sisters and in what was often the custom our mother used to dress us up in sailor suits, a patriotic gesture, which was not uncommon in those days.

I remember boarding a tram in Barrow-in-Furness in my sailor suit when a passenger in real naval uniform greeted me "Hello Jack Tar!" he said, as I took my seat. The town of Barrow was resplendent with naval uniforms of all ranks from officers to men commissioning their ships which were built by the well

(*l to r*) In my first naval uniform with my three sisters: Stella, Pat and Joan; Barrow-in-Furness, Cumbria, 1917

known firm Messrs Vickers-Armstrong Limited, Naval Construction Works, of which my father was the Gun-mounting Manager.

I was so impressed by the honour of recognition by a real Jack Tar that my mother asked me if I would like the nickname 'Jack'? Highly delighted I retained this name until the age of 10, when I was sent to a boarding school where I reverted to my proper name of Allan.

One of my main Great War memories was when I was five while I was having a bath. It was reported that an airship was flying close to our house trailing a rope. Apparently it appeared to be in trouble. My nanny returned to the bathroom to find me standing on the window sill completely naked enjoying the wonderful view of the airship in its predicament. I was rapidly snatched from the otherwise alarming counter spectacle I presented to our neighbours! I was teased for this event, by the family for years to come.

While on this subject, and as the aftermath of German airship bombing raids on London during the Great War, the British Government had given the firm Vickers-Armstrong in Barrow an order to build airships for experimental reasons; and this was one of their early models. More I do not know, as I was only 5 at the time, except that I remember well the later tragedy of the R101,

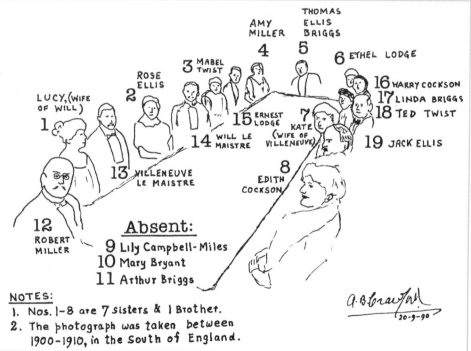

AMY MILLER

THOMAS ELLIS BRIGGS

4 5

3 MABEL TWIST

6 ETHEL LODGE

ROSE ELLIS

2

16 HARRY COCKSON
17 LINDA BRIGGS
18 TED TWIST

LUCY, (WIFE OF WILL)

1

15 ERNEST LODGE

7 KATE (WIFE OF VILLENEUVE)

14 WILL LE MAISTRE

19 JACK ELLIS

13 VILLENEUVE LE MAISTRE

8 EDITH COCKSON

12 ROBERT MILLER

Absent:

9 Lily Campbell-Miles
10 Mary Bryant
11 Arthur Briggs

NOTES:
1. Nos. 1-8 are 7 sisters & 1 Brother.
2. The photograph was taken between 1900-1910, in the South of England.

a.B.Crawford
20-9-90

Great Aunt Amy Miller, wife of Robert Miller, was the one who left me a small legacy. Seven of my great aunts were all sisters and all were married. The dinner above shows a first course of oysters, arranged to celebrate some occasion around 1910, near the south coast, the whereabouts unknown. Ironically, my own grandmother, Mary Bryant, could not be present for the occasion which is believed to be because of a problem with transport from Cheshire. The eight married sisters had one brother who is sitting at the head of the table.

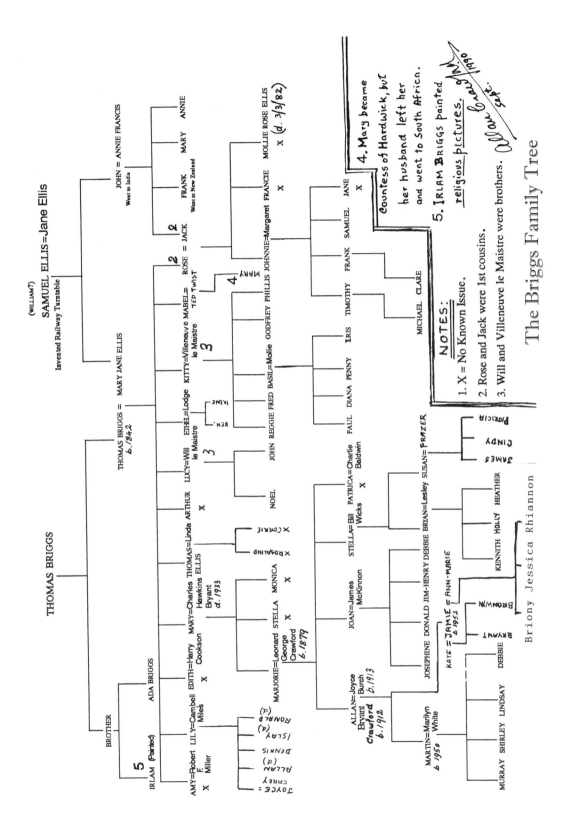

The Briggs Family Tree

Briony Jessica Rhiannon

The Briggs Family Tree

The discovery of the photograph of the Briggs Family Reunion Dinner, together with other old family records which I had, enabled me to form a more complete picture of our ancestors, and to document it before all was lost.

Bill Wicks found the portrait of the 3-year old Thomas Briggs abandoned amongst the late Mollie Ellis' effects and took an excellent photograph of this picture: this photograph introduces the series.

Thomas and Mary Briggs had 11 children shown clearly in the family tree overleaf. There were 2 sons and 9 daughters – all nine of whom were married.

Seven of these daughters, and the son Thomas Ellis Briggs, are all shown in the Family Reunion Dinner, together with their spouses. Most of them can be identified amongst the individual photographs which are also included in this collection.

Of the 11 Briggs children, Arthur, Lily (Elizabeth) and Mary and their spouses were not present. Nothing is known about Arthur, but Lily, who married Adolphus Campbell-Miles. and their 5 children were in Canada at the time. This information I acquired from their daughter Joyce Carey, whom my wife and I visited in the village of Southwick near Portsmouth in 1989.

She was in her 90th year and looked good for another 10 years (she had run a market garden for many years in the same area).

Also absent from the photograph are my grandmother (Mary) and grandfather (Charles Bryant). She and her husband were of a retiring disposition and the journey from Cheshire or North Wales to the south of England may have been too much for them. On the other hand, ill-health or pregnancy may have caused their absence.

As far as I can recollect, the Briggs family lived in the Manchester area as so many photographs were taken there.

We Crawford grandchildren of Mary knew well four of those in the Reunion photograph; Robert and Amy Miller, Jack and Rosie Ellis.

I understood from Aunt Amy that the Briggs family originated from Hazelalack near Arnside in North Lancashire, and this prompted me to photograph the 'Castle' remains during my apprenticeship days at Barrow-in-Furness.

After Mary Briggs died, Thomas married the housekeeper and had 4 or 5 more children – not recognised by the rest of the family.

an airship that set out from England for India in 1930. She was constructed in Cardington, Bedfordshire and was supposed to be bigger and better than any designed in the world before. She ended in tragedy the following day in flames with the death of almost everyone on board. It was near Beauvais, in France a few hours after her departure. The R100 which was built at Barrow was smaller but had been across to Canada and back successfully. As a result of government policy the manufacture of airships with rigid frames was abandoned for good and the R100 went to the breaker's yard.

Though not involved in the airship branch of his firm, my father occupied a responsible position but after the end of the 1914-1918 war, there was less work for shipbuilding firms and he, like many of the employees, was declared redundant and had to find another job.

~~~~

We lived economically for a while in a tiny country house at a place called Woodland in North Lancashire at a halt on the Coniston branch railway line. Occasionally, when we went shopping in the nearby village of Broughton I, as an enthusiastic youngster would travel to the village in the engine, and return home in the guard's van. This diversity resulted in my interest in matters of engineering which developed later in life.

My first school from the age of 8 to 10 was "Sunny Brae" School for Girls, which had a half a dozen boys under 10. It was situated in the beautiful village of Grange-over-Sands in Cumbria and although perfectly happy there I remember little about the school.

Eventually my father succeeded in being appointed to an armaments factory in Kirkee, Poona, India. This meant that from 1922-1927 I was lucky enough to be sent to a good prep boarding school called *The Craig*, at Windermere within a mile or two of the lake. It was a very good preparatory school run by the headmaster Mr William Snow and teachers several of whom had distinguished themselves one way or another at Oxford University, either in sports or academics.

Although I was in the cricket and football teams I never distinguished myself academically but I did win a gardening prize! I was not a reader and had a dyslexic problem that the headmaster tried to rectify by making me read aloud to him every morning for several months while waiting for breakfast. It was a happy school but I did not like the quick cold baths we were compelled to take before breakfast in the summer term. We learnt to swim in Lake Windermere attached to a rope on the end of a pole held by a master on the end of a pier. It was safe and reasonably effective.

Our most famous pupil was W. W. Wakefield who captained England's rugby team in his day and later became a Member of Parliament. This was before my time. All my life I have been grateful to my parents for having sent me to such a good school. I know it was a great financial burden for them with three daughters to consider as well as myself.

In 1926, at the age of 13, my parents had already decided to enter me for the Royal Naval College at Dartmouth; and so, I was sent up to London to sit for the naval exam. My Aunt Stella Bryant and Great Aunt Amy Miller of Barrow hosted me in London as this was a great event. A panel of men interviewed me, amongst whom we were told was a real Admiral. I am glad to say I passed this venture but, sorry to report, on my second visit to London to write the further examinations I had not been warned I would have to write a French *dictée*. I could not write a single word and handed in a blank sheet of paper! Of course I failed and did not go to Dartmouth. The Navy, I gathered, was not for me. I was not unduly worried but my parents were very disappointed.

In 1927 I was transferred from The Craig to the public school Wellington near Taunton in Somerset, which was good at caring for students who had parents on service overseas. I stayed there until I was 18. The school was well run by headmaster George Corner, his wife and his sister Miss Corner who took a great interest in the welfare of the boys of absent parents. George Corner was very creatively orientated and had his own powerhouse to produce electricity. Although a very quiet and otherwise trouble free student, I was, I think the only boy who had had as many as two canings from the headmaster!

My misdeeds however were not all that shameful: The first was caused as a result of my great interest in listening to the radio. I listened in on a crystal set which gave free reception. I could listen in to *London Calling* by twiddling what we called a cat's whisker on to a crystal, with old-fashioned headphones on one's head. This process cost nothing but was superseded by a radio valve and a battery. This was a great advance but the batteries required charging. I learnt to charge my batteries by passing an electric current through the battery. I did this by surreptitiously hiding an electric light bulb in a box in a cupboard in the corner of the powerhouse. The current passing through the bulb heated it to such an extent that it ignited the cupboard and set it on fire, threatening to burn down the whole powerhouse. George Corner fortunately spotted the danger just in time; he must have seen me fiddling around the cupboard and afterwards demanded my presence for six strokes on the backside.

Fortunately this did not affect our relationship which was cordial at all times and I even helped him doing odd jobs in connection with his construction of a Memorial Chapel in memory of students killed in the 1914-1918 war. George

Corner personally carved most of the oak pew-ends.

The second occasion of caning arose quite unexpectedly. My three sisters spent a couple of terms at the Blackdown School for Girls, which was fairly close to Wellington School for Boys. I visited them surreptitiously on one or two occasions chatting over an adjoining fence in a neighbouring orchard. I don't remember stealing apples, but the neighbour reported this to the headmaster who realised it was me and gave me six more on the *derrière*. Again this did not affect our relationship and he gave me a very good 'To whom it may concern' at the end of my school days.

My parents continued their presence in India but pressed on trying to get me into the Navy and they recommended I should have another whack at this by entering what was known as the Special Entry at the age of 18. I cannot recollect much about this exam other than that I failed again, this time because I had not been entered to write the subject 'lower mathematics'. I was NOT destined, I thought, for the Navy!

~~~

My last term at school was the summer term of 1930. In 1931 my parents returned from India and we settled in Cornwall for our permanent home. Firstly we lived at a remote place called Draynes, near Liskeard; then we moved to Scorrier near Truro. Then mother moved us to St Agnes on the north coast where we lived in the old harbour master's cottage by the sea. The local people called it 'Mr Hitchin's used-to-be'! A previous harbour master had installed a bath in the greenhouse and so, when the grapes ripened they dangled temptingly over one's head while performing one's ablutions!

I started to lose count of our whereabouts as my mother had a thing about moving; she saw a lovely cottage, bought it and was then ready to move on. In 1937 when I sailed from Southampton to Cape Town in South Africa looking for a job, our new home in Cornwall was in a lovely house called Treviskey near Gwennap, three miles southeast from the old town of Redruth. But my parents moved once more ending up at Port Isaac on the north coast.

By November 1948, while I was still in South Africa, father's life ended at the age of 69 and he was buried in St Endellion churchyard in close proximity within the area. My mother ended her days in 1956 in the nearby village of Chapel Amble in dramatic fashion.

Engineering Apprenticeship

Due to my interest in engineering my father and I went up to Barrow-in-Furness and arrangements were made for me to enter the firm Vickers-Armstrong as a nominated apprentice. I would study three years in the various workshops from pattern making to fitting shops, followed by two years in the drawing offices. At the end of five years, provided I passed night school exams at the local technical college I would have completed my apprenticeship and gained my indentures.

I started my engineering apprenticeship in Barrow-in-Furness in 1931 and I have never forgotten the Burnett family who took me under their wing. He was the Borough Electrical Engineer. Their great friends were the Rev. and Mrs Stannard who was the vicar of St John's Church and whose rectory was so large that they offered Vickers-Armstrong Ltd accommodation for a well-behaved apprentice. I fancy they had in mind a possible built-in babysitter as an added asset to any arrangement they could make and I dare say my father's thoughts were that I could be kept on the straight and narrow if I could board in such an environment. Father was an ex-employee of the firm, so we made straight for the Stannards when looking on the list of 'digs' in the area when we arrived there at the start of my engineering apprenticeship. Sadly, the vacancy had already been filled, but their acquaintance had been made which was a good introduction. My family and theirs remained friends for many years to come.

I lived in 'digs' for which my parents paid, although apprentices did receive low weekly wages which helped.

It was wonderful to be free and able to live my own life. I was very shy during my twenties and never had a girlfriend; but once I left home and became independent, I joined clubs and made several very good family friends. I contacted friends I had made in my prep school days and played golf, tennis and even joined a badminton club.

I shared my digs with a friend Ian Toler from Cheshire who was a leading figure in the Territorial Army and in World War II joined the Glider Pilot Regiment, earning the DFC. He worked in the local steel works. The local vicar and his wife were great friends who influenced my future life very significantly.

~~~

By special arrangement with Vickers-Armstrong Ltd and the German firm Biernatzki & Co. of Chemnitz, Saxony, it was agreed that one of my five years apprenticeship would be spent with them in Germany. They manufactured metal milling machines and specialised in machines that created the centre part of typewriters with all the slots that held the letters and characters.

I spent six months in the workshops and six months in the drawing office. I knew not a word of German but was glad to have a year of study there. I witnessed the development of Nazi Germany and was glad to be a foreigner.

At a restaurant in Munich railway station I sat at a table for breakfast with a man, his wife and daughter. It was clear to me they were anti the present Nazi regime and were very friendly. He was a professor who specialised in mushrooms which he had studied in World War One when, as he said, the Americans and the British were trying to starve the Germans during hostilities. They lived in Potsdam and invited me to stay with them for a weekend during the 1936 Olympic Games where I witnessed Jesse Owen win the 100 metre sprint and Hitler refusing to shake Owen's hand as he was black!

Another incident I remember happened in the drawing office at the firm Biernatzki & Co. On arrival every morning, the employees greeted their colleagues 'Heil Hitler'. My greeting however, was 'Grüss Gott'! One German colleague of mine didn't like this and one day, in my drawer, I found a note containing a poem he had written virtually saying that when one is a guest in Germany, one should raise his arm and greet 'Heil Hitler'! I reported this to the Managing Director's son, Herbert. He replied, "Don't worry Allan. That is a 'kleiner Hitler'. There are a lot of them around."

It was a wonderful opportunity for me to have been selected to study for a year in Germany in spite of all the publicity associated with the Nazi regime. To emphasise the good from the bad, I learnt quite a number of German songs which helped me with the language and I was able in my time to visit some beautiful country districts like the Black Forest, the Bastei – a scenic area on the river Elbe – and the potteries at the famous town of Meissen, not far from Dresden. At weekends during winter months a group of expatriates used to take a bus to the Fichtelgebirge in Czechoslovakia where we learnt to ski, far from the madding crowds of marching Nazi paramilitary groups!

On one occasion a Swedish friend Sven Stähle and I went round the art galleries one morning in Dresden and saw what we were told was the most famous picture in the world – the Sixtinische Madonna by Raffael, painted in the 1500's. It was a magnificent work of art. I bought a postcard of it, and recorded the date of our visit on the back, which was 10-6-1935. I stowed it away in my

Sixtinische Madonna by Raffael

records and never recovered it until accidentally on 9-6-2005, within one day of the 70 years it had remained in hiding! The coincidence of the date was pointed out to me by my dentist friend Elizabeth Evans to whom I showed the postcard. She subsequently happened to visit the area in central Italy where Raffael had worked when he did the painting over 500 years before. She found an anthology in the bedroom of the house in which she sojourned, which reported that these valuable works of art had been sent to the U.S.S.R. for safekeeping during WWII and were returned to Dresden when the art galleries had been rebuilt in peacetime.

I returned to England once I had qualified for my apprenticeship whereupon I decided to leave again to branch out to one of the Dominions, where life was less restricted. I chose South Africa as students in Barrow had told me there was great scope for engineers in that country.

4

A First-Class Encounter

This was where my great-aunt Amy came into play for she had left my three sisters and me small, but very welcome, legacies, which greatly helped to arrange our holidays. I was not to know it at the time but the whole course of my life was altered by her kind bequest.

It was for a reason at that time unknown to me, that I was motivated to use the legacy to buy a first-class single ticket on the mail-ship *Arundel Castle*, bound from Southampton to Cape Town, in December, 1937.

I soon made friends with a fellow passenger, Robin Williams of Kimberley who was returning home after his degree in engineering at Cambridge. It was coincidence that we met and enjoyed the company of Dr Erling Christophersen, Curator of the Botanical Museum in Oslo, Norway.

The chance meeting with Dr Christophersen added greatly to the interest of the voyage, for his personality and companionship were qualifications worthy of acquaintance.

One day he informed me that he was bound for Tristan da Cunha, where he was leading a party of a dozen fellow Norwegians on an expedition to study the various branches of science in which they were interested. He also revealed that Tristan island had never been properly surveyed and that he had not been able to acquire a surveyor. On hearing this, I jokingly volunteered, even though I knew nothing of survey work and, to my amazement, he took me seriously and I was accepted.

Dr Erling Christophersen

Robin Williams subsequently helped me to revise my trigonometry and taught me how to survey during the rest of our voyage to Cape Town. I also learnt more about Tristan and the Norwegian connection.

During the 19th Century sealing and whaling were industries that flourished in the South Atlantic and circumpolar seas of the southern hemisphere. United States whaling vessels were common as they learnt that vast stocks of whales were to be encountered. Trading in seal skins as

well as whale oil presented a good investment. American as well as European countries were joined by Norwegians and South American companies as interest in the industry developed. Propulsion of ships changed from sailing ships to coal, and from coal to oil fired vessels. During this development period when whale blubber was originally "tryed out" in boilers based on shore (like South Georgia) large ships known as "Whale Factory Ships" were constructed which were attended by sometimes as many as 6 or 10 "catchers" to hunt the whales. These brought the catch to the factory ships which processed the blubber on board, storing the oil in tanks in place of barrels. The firm Thor Dahl of Sandefjord, Norway was a shipping company that built several "Whale Factory Ships" of several thousand tons each to process whale oil. These ships with names like *Thorshammer* and *Thorshovdi* each accompanied by the 300 ton catchers frequented the waters of the southern hemisphere during the summer months. Quite often they anchored off Tristan da Cunha on their passage south or north.

It was the managing director of the company Thor Dahl, Consul Lars Christensen, who, after a boring few months in the ice fields spotted the verdant slopes of Gough Island, 200 miles south of Tristan da Cunha. He was tempted to go ashore. Interested in botany he made a quick collection of several specimens which he carefully took back to Norway. He presented them to Dr Erling Christophersen, Curator of the Botanical Museum, Oslo, for classification. Christophersen reported half a dozen new species previously unknown to science in that area. As he had spent several years previously on scientific work in the Pacific Ocean, it was realised that an expedition to Tristan da Cunha (which had never been worked by scientists) could reveal interesting results.

Consul Christensen was quick to seek the British Government's permission to visit the island for scientific research and Dr Erling Christophersen was appointed leader. Christensen as sponsor

My friend, Robin Williams, whom I met on board the *Arundel Castle* in 1937.

21

undertook transport costs in his Whale Factory Ships and H.R.H. Crown Prince Olav of Norway agreed to be Patron. Ten Norwegian scientists were chosen as members of the party which included biologists, a doctor, dentist, factotum, etc., etc. and spent four months on the island.

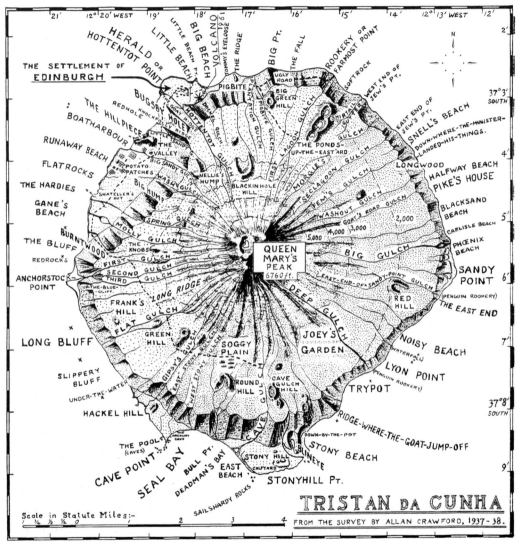

Tristan da Cunha *(ABC, 1937-38)*

The Naming of
Queen Mary's Peak

When I landed on Tristan Island for the first time in 1937, as the Surveyor of the Norwegian Scientific Exhibition, I noticed that not many of the names on the Admiralty chart corresponded with the names used by the local islander population. It was at once evident that I should record the actual names used by the inhabitants for all topographical features in order to produce a meaningful chart.

To think back to December 1937 when I was rowed ashore in a canvas boat manned by a crew of silent islanders, one man spoke after I had announced that I was an Englishman and the rest of our party were Norwegians. The man at stroke eventually broke silence by asking:

"How's the King and Queen?"

"They are very well, thank you" I replied – making myself responsible for their Majesties' well being!

"Was they crowned?" I was further asked, for this was the welfare of King George VI and Queen Elizabeth later to be known as the Queen Mother. I was impressed by the islanders' loyalty towards the Royal Family, for many of the island cottages displayed their photographs especially King George V and his consort. In fact Queen Mary had taken a great interest in the islanders welfare and had presented the community with a harmonium for their Church.

The collection of names was an interesting procedure. No names had ever been deliberately given: they were either a natural description of a place like Big Green Hill, Sandy Point or Seal Bay for example, or the name used was the recollection of an incident that had taken place at a particular area, like Frank's Hill (where a visiting sailor was benighted on his meanderings) or Anchorstock Point (where the wooden stock of a sailing ship's anchor was washed ashore). This particular name is the natural contraction of the original more cumbersome name 'The beach where the Anchorstock washed up'! There are still a couple of long names in use which reflect their natural descriptive form –'Down where the Minister land his things'. In 1906 when Rev. and Mrs Barrow arrived for a three-year chaplaincy, the weather was too rough to land at the Settlement so they chose a beach landing in the lee. To this day the beach is still known as 'Down where the Minister land his things'. It is because the name goes with a swing that it is still in general use; but it is a small beach not significant enough to tempt a Naval Hydrographer to use it on an official chart!

There is already a Goat Ridge on the west side of the village, so a ridge on the south of the island is known as the 'Ridge-where-the-goat-jump-off' the sentence being used ungrammatically in full (they seldom used the past tense in speech). I collected over 80 names around the coast altogether. The islanders never convened a meeting with the intention of naming this or that particular place, all names being natural derivations of one sort or another.

My fieldwork was all recorded by triangulation and I carried out almost a complete coastline traverse. After 4 months I was picked up unexpectedly by Escort Vessel *H.M.S. Milford*, which took me (via Gough Island) to Simonstown the naval base in South Africa, home of the Commander-in-Chief South Atlantic Rear-Admiral D'Oyly Lyon, R.N. Here they took me under their wing and the Fleet Navigational Officer was appointed to make sure that I drew up my 'fair chart' in the approved naval manner. I was informed that if any important topographical feature on the chart did not have a name, as the surveyor of virgin territory I was entitled to allocate suitable names of my choice. I allocated the names *Gane* and *Snell* to unnamed beaches to commemorate island benefactors and a headland on the south east of the island *Lyon Point* after the admiral whose staff had helped me so much.

Queen Mary
(*courtesy Royal Archives, Windsor Castle*)

As the peak of the island, highest point 6760 feet (2060 metres) above sea level was unnamed, I thought at once of naming it *Queen Mary's Peak*. The highest point of Tenerife Island was named Pico de Teide and I thought Tristan's highest point worthy of a name of its own!

Her Majesty was kept updated about the welfare of Tristan da Cunha by the famous British General Sir Reginald Wingate who had made his name in Egypt and the Sudan during the late 1800's. I got to know him quite well through my shipboard friend, Robin Williams. Any news I had from Tristan, General Wingate passed on to H.M The Queen through a lady-in-waiting. He even sent a pair of island homespun knitted socks for

To
my friend Allan Crawford
whose distinguished service in
Tristan da Cunha and
Marion Island have earned
him well-deserved recognition
from
Reginald Wingate (General).

Her Majesty's inspection on one occasion!

After 4 months on Tristan I eventually completed the survey.

By 1938 I had already placed her name on my fair chart when it was signed and approved by the Admiral; it was then sent to Norway for Dr. Christophersen's signature, as Leader of the Expedition. Reference to the fair chart reveals I had also named a smaller peak 'Mount Olav' after the Crown Prince of Norway, who was patron of our expedition but no comment was forthcoming about that event – it had never been observed as far as I know.

Christophersen then sent the chart to England to the Naval Hydrographer for updating of chart No. 1769. I had produced the first authentic chart of Tristan Island which was used by the British Admiralty. The story of the success of the 4-month sojourn of the expedition's visit has been told in several books and large volumes of research have been recorded by the scientists.

One day I will write to the Hydrographer in Taunton to ask him if he would kindly consider entering the name Queen Mary's Peak on the appropriate chart.

~~~

The Norwegians were due to go back to Norway by way of the whale factory ship *Thorshammer* which was due call on 29 March 1938. I was to embark with them as this was my only known way to return to South Africa via the northern hemisphere as *Thorshammer* was not scheduled to call anywhere in the southern hemisphere after leaving Tristan. However, Captain R.L.B. Cunliffe R.N. arrived unexpectedly at Tristan in *H.M.S. Milford* the day before the *Thorshammer.* My request for a lift direct to the Cape was graciously agreed for 28 March.

The object of Captain Cunliffe's visit to Tristan was in order to present on behalf of the British Government an Order in Council to the inhabitants of Tristan proclaiming them and their Island Dependencies subjects of the Governor of St Helena, as this had never been officially arranged before. Indeed on the morrow he was due to sail to uninhabited Gough Island 230 sea miles south of Tristan to be declared within the same Dependency and to plant the Union Jack

HMS Milford and the Union flag on Gough Island
(*photos: ABC*)

there as proof of British ownership! By granting me passage in his ship, I was enabled to witness this very unusual ceremony on the following day.

We arrived a week later in Simon's Town, South Africa when the Royal Navy took me under their wing because they realised I had been indirectly working for them providing information useful by having surveyed British Territory previously only sketched from the sea. They gave me a month's accommodation in a vacant cabin on board a ship in the dockyard, an office ashore in which to work providing me with instruments and materials to draw my charts, all this under the supervision of the Fleet Navigation Officer. No one at that time realised how useful this chart would be to the Allied Cause when hostilities broke out in 1939. The Island was later used in 1942 on which to build a naval communications shore-base.

The village of Edinburgh (*photo Debbie Crawford, 2004*)

King Olav V of Norway (*courtesy Royal Palace, Oslo*)

In 1987, six of us celebrated the 50th Anniversary of our landing on Tristan da Cunha with a special lunch in Oslo, prior to which we took coffee with King Olav V in the Royal Palace: in 1937 he had been the Patron of our Expedition – 50 years earlier!

One of the major successes of the Norwegian Scientific Expedition has been the research work carried out at the island by marine biologist Erling Sivertsen who forecast the validity of establishing a crayfishing industry for the island, an event which was successfully established from Cape Town in 1949 and is in operation until this day. The island's economy is based on the royalties derived therefrom and from the sale of postage stamps and local crafts.

Painting by the late George Pilkington of Cave Point, on the south west of Tristan Island,
(*reproduced from a photograph I took in 1938*)

Marigens patches, still abandoned but now island property. In 1938 they were legally mine, according to island custom, as I bartered them for a pair of trousers from Henry Green on my first visit to Tristan da Cunha. When I returned in 1946 I planted potatoes and vegetables in one patch but the produce was not worthwhile. (*photo Debbie Crawford 2004*)

6

"A Fine Romance, My Friend This Is"

When I went to live and work in Pretoria in 1939, I made the acquaintance of Lenchen, who was a petite and vivacious girl, in fact, I had never met in my life anyone like her before. Sadly, she was married and it turned out that she was ten years my senior!

Lenchen was a charming lady with whom I fell in platonic love, hook, line and sinker and I must emphasise that it was a perfectly platonic relationship. If this had not happened, I might have taken a wrong turn and not been around to write my memoirs which is more like the introduction to a drama than to a romance.

All the participants who were involved, except me, have passed on, hopefully to a better world. It is only the nickname of the principal character that is revealed as this appears on the endorsement of my very first book.

~~~

Lenchen had her own charming family, but this was not to deter our occasional meeting in the centre of Pretoria at our favourite café; nor for that matter, once in a while when we drove into the country to a restaurant called 'Fountains' where we sat outdoors to enjoy the natural environment. Being only human I remember I once tried to nudge up to her to get close but this shrewd personality repelled my approach with the determined command "Get back into your box" which of course I did, never to make the same mistake again!

I was staying with mutual friends in a private house in a residential area known as Waterkloof and one day when I returned to my hostess' home I found that the lock of a little leather box in which I kept my diary had been forced open! My activities (probably vis-à-vis my latest friend) had aroused suspicion and I was so incensed that I gave notice and left.

I changed my boarding arrangements to Windsor House in the vicinity of the Union Buildings also in a pleasant residential area of the city. And it was, in this private boarding house to which I had just moved, that I chanced to meet a Royal Naval Liaison officer from Simon's Town. He had been instructed to locate me in Pretoria and to request a confidential report on navigational and onshore conditions on a certain area in the middle of the South Atlantic Ocean. What a coincidence! I soon supplied the requested report which I posted forthwith.

An interesting incident happened in the vicinity of Lenchen's home near which I was passing in my small car in the hope, I must admit, that I might spot her. Instead I noticed a young lady in distress and stopped to see if I could help. To my amazement it was Lenchen, crying, as the result of some misunderstanding she had had at home. I did not enquire as to the reason, but our relationship was not weakened, on the contrary, it was strengthened by this event.

She knew I had visited Tristan da Cunha in 1938 and had written the book *I Went To Tristan* which was published in London. Being wartime it was delayed but expected any day soon to be exported to South Africa. We were walking outside a bookshop on our way to our favourite café when she spotted a copy of my book on display in the window. In great excitement we entered the shop and she bought this first copy, which I endorsed to her there and then with the following inscription:

> *"To Lenchen*
> *with much love from the author Allan.*
> *This is the first copy*
> *of the first edition*
> *of my first book.*
> *Pretoria, May 1941"*

What an optimist indeed I was. It was certainly my first book but although I eventually wrote four more books in later life, they were *all* first editions.

~~~

There is a postscript to this story of romance. In 1941 Lenchen must have been talking in her sleep or perhaps extolling the success of my book. One day her husband, out of the blue, invited me to call at his office in the centre of Pretoria. I was completely mystified, as I was innocent of any iniquitous activity, and like a lamb to its slaughter I arrived wondering what the reason could be.

I knocked on the door, which he opened and closed behind me. He then produced a revolver! I did not panic but he offered it to me. Still in complete ignorance I proclaimed my disinterest in such a weapon and for a flash moment I wondered if this was an invitation to a duel at dawn, or whether he was suggesting I should use it on myself, or on him. I quickly sidled towards the door emphasising once more my disinterest in the weapon and made my escape. I never heard anything more!

~~~

In November 1941 I left the steelworks and, all rigged up in my new Air Force uniform, I left Pretoria station by train for Port Elizabeth to begin my wartime active service. I was seen off by two good friends Reg and Madeline Pettit and, of course my dear old friend of all time, Lenchen. It was very sad to cut short the life in which I had doted for so long. She gave me two useful farewell presents, which I still have to this day, after over 60 years. One was a good quality zip wallet for my passport and birth certificate and the other was a strong wooden security box in which to conserve my photographic equipment, diaries and other valuables.

Ultimately I realised how fortunate I had been to have had such a 'fine romance' for if it had not been for the natural restrictions as the consequence of her friendship, I am convinced my life would not have developed in the unique way in which it did.

~~~~

There is an aftermath to the story of the 'first copy of my first book' which extends into the 21st Century.

One day, in November 2004, a friend, Michael D Mueller of Morgantown, West Virginia, wrote to advise me a copy of the book *I Went To Tristan* had turned up on the Internet for sale with the exact endorsement I had written to Lenchen. It was the very same book Lenchen had bought, and supposedly after her death some years ago had appeared on the second-hand book market. It was advertised for over $200, a price Mike Mueller regarded as excessive. My typist Karen Marr discovered the same information on the Internet in June 2005 but when I decided to buy it for Debbie, one of my granddaughters, Karen informed me the vendor had announced that the copy had been lost or misfiled and was unobtainable, and could no longer be traced. A sad ending to the story, or so we thought!

However in September 2005 we received a communication from Johannesburg to say they had found the book, which had been misfiled under the category 'Music', and were we still interested? A quick affirmative reply resulted in a message from my granddaughter Debbie in Cape Town who informed me she received the copy of the book on 20 September with the remark "Wow, I feel extremely privileged to have a complete signed collection of all four of your books, Grandad!"

One Way to Join the Navy!

aving failed two attempts to join the Royal Navy from two different schools the next stage in my naval saga may sound ironic, for to achieve this ultimate destiny was completely unknown to me at that present time.

It was in 1941 during World War II, which was already in progress. As a qualified engineer I was engaged in a reserved occupation and unable to leave the steel works in Pretoria. A request came through for me from the Directorate of Manpower to join the South African Air Force in its meteorological section in order to help the Royal Navy to establish a shore-based naval weather and communications station in a secret locality. It turned out to be on Tristan da Cunha. I was the only person in Africa at the time that had local knowledge of the area.

Naval communication and weather stations were established on the island in 1942. Known secretly as *H.M.S. Job 9* it was later renamed *H.M.S. Atlantic Isle* in 1944. The shore-based naval ship was abandoned two years later when it was taken over by civilian authorities. The events of this episode are reported in my

> I, Surgeon Lieutenant-Commander E.J.S. Woolley R.N.V.R.,M.O.i/c and
>
> MAGISTRATE of this Island of TRISTAN da CUNHA, do hereby appoint you
>
> *Alan B. CRAWFORD* a COUNCILLOR for the period of one year.
>
> You will act as my adviser and do hereby receive AUTHORITY TO ENFORCE
>
> UNDER MY DIRECTION, the LAW , ORDER and CUSTOM of this Island, including
>
> any FUTURE ORDERS and ARRANGEMENTS we may make.
>
> *[signature]*
>
> [stamp: MEDICAL OFFICER-IN-CHARGE / 6 NOV 1942 / TRISTAN DA CUNHA]

last book, *Tristan da Cunha: Wartime Invasion*, published in 2004 from notes and diaries I had kept in the period 1942-48.

I joined the Air Force, had a quick course in meteorology and was seconded to the Royal Navy for 2 years, being stationed firstly in Simonstown then in May 1942 on Tristan da Cunha under Surgeon Lieutenant-Commander E J S Woolley R.N.V.R. for most of that time until 1943, as their weather man.

I also served as a sort of liaison between the islanders and the Navy; and to carry out my duties effectively the Doctor appointed me as an island councillor for one year. My main job alongside my meteorological work was to create a local home guard consisting of 16 island men who were issued with rifles, helmets, ammunition and were trained to act in an emergency. They resembled 'Dad' Army'.

The 16 members of the Tristan Defence Volunteers (TDV)
(Photograph given to me by a friend whose name I have sadly forgotten, who served after I left in 1943)

I returned to Tristan in 1946 to take over the naval establishment on behalf of the South African Weather Bureau whose organisation I had joined as a meteorologist when I was demobilised.

It was because of my continued contact with the Royal Navy and my acquired knowledge of maritime affairs that I was appointed to a new post in the Cape Town Docks entitled Port Meteorological Officer. The World Meteorological Organisation in Geneva, Switzerland recommended appointments of this nature.

The World Meteorological Organisation was an International Organisation formed like the United Nations that had a branch called the Commission for Maritime Meteorology. I was fortunate in being appointed by the South African

Weather Bureau as their representative on this Commission. My office in Cape Town Docks was placed in the then R.N.V.R. (SA Division) Naval Base. This was convenient for I had a permanent government car on loan to enable me to visit ships to organise their weather reports by radio when they sailed away. This greatly improved the quality of the weather forecasts they would be able to read as they proceeded on their voyages. This ideal arrangement was intended to cover all the oceans of the world but may by now have been superseded by more modern satellite technology.

~~~~

During hostilities I included the names of two old great aunts of mine, Maude and Lilly Miller, in a list of recipients to whom I sent food parcels, to supplement their meagre wartime rations. They were in fact the unmarried sisters of my great uncle Robert Miller, husband of great aunt Amy, who left me the legacy which altered the whole of my life. My aunts had moved from Grange-over-Sands, Cumbria, to Bexhill-on-Sea on the Sussex coast where the climate was warmer and had adopted me as a sort of surrogate nephew.

My aunts knew that before WWII I had visited Tristan and made a survey. They studied the few books that existed on the history of that Island and were fascinated to learn that the Rev. Edwin Dodgson, brother of the author Lewis Carroll, had spent several years during the 1880's on the Island caring for the well-being and spiritual interests of the local inhabitants. They were keen for me to visit them in England should I be able to return. Thinking of Lewis Carroll's connection with his brother on Tristan, they composed a parody based on his poem *You are old father William* from the book *Alice in Wonderland*.

The Wanderer's Return (circa 1950)

1

"You are late Nephew Allan," the old aunts cried,
"We've expected you day after day!
But instead you've been wandering far and wide
Now what is the reason we pray?"

2

"You're still hale and hearty, dear aunties, I know,
Though I'm sorry I couldn't come sooner,
But the call of my country compelled me to go
To the island of Tristan da Cunha!"

3

"You were bold Nephew Allan – now what did you do
On the loneliest isle in the world?"
"Oh, I climbed up the highlands and made a survey
And the banner of Britain unfurled!"

4

"Well done," the old aunties in unison cried,
"But weren't the wild natives molesting?"
"Far from it: I might have selected a bride!
The fair ones were so interesting!"

5

"And while with the men I was climbing the rocks
The women were busily knitting,
Their home-woven wool into stockings and socks
To present to the stranger on quitting!"

6

"We are old nephew Allan, but young in our hearts
And the tales of your travels delight us.
The tigers and elephants, swamps and escapes
Combine to instruct and excite us!"

7

"When you finally cease roaming and birdlike come homing,
Young Crusoe at last to 'Wood Lea',
In bath chairs side-by-side your old aunts, with glad pride,
Will welcome you back for your tea!"

The lure eventually worked and after my marriage and a family of 2 sons, I returned to England in the early 1950's and visited my old aunts again. Aunt Lilly died in 1956 at the age of 102, her sister a few years earlier.

~~~~

One day at a cocktail party not long after the war, Commodore F J Dean OBE, the former Head of the South African Navy, asked me if I would like to join the R.N.V.R. (SA Division) as a volunteer. I would have the rank of Lieutenant in the Special Branch as a meteorologist. This was for me a great opportunity and I was soon to accept the offer. It involved a weekly 'parade' when shipmates assembled at the base known as *S.A.S. Unitie* in Cape Town Docks, receiving instruction in Naval affairs. I studied codes and cyphers. One could also promulgate one's own expertise, like possibly in my case 'weather'. One was also expected to spend some time at sea, and I saw at once this might enable me to visit some of my favourite island outposts.

After a couple of years I was sent overseas to the United Kingdom to attend a five month Royal Naval Weather Forecasting Course in Meteorology at *HMS Harrier* in Pembrokeshire. Specialists selected to attend courses were flown over to Europe in South African Anson transport aircraft which could only fly during daylight hours. We stopped in different countries along the route, this being before restrictions were imposed on South African aircraft prohibiting landings in Africa because of the country's out-dated apartheid policy.

The course at *HMS Harrier* was successfully completed but there was a special personal family interest in my return visit to the land of my birth. After all the efforts of my parents to get me into the Royal Navy in my youth had failed, I had unexpectedly in adulthood been invited into officer status in that self-same Navy! I naturally was looking forward to presenting myself to my mother whom I had not seen for several years, as she was still living in Cornwall. My father had died a few years earlier. My wife and two sons were following by sea as I also planned for my mother to meet them.

~~~~

Unexpected drama awaited me on arrival in the UK. We landed at Northolt Aerodrome and hearing by telephone my mother was not able to meet my train on the following day I took a taxi from Wadebridge Station to the nice little cottage at Chapel Amble which was the village in which she lived. It was a joy to find she appeared to be reasonably well and we spent many hours recounting past recollections. I told her of my wife's imminent arrival with her two grandsons by sea, whom she had never met. It was after midnight when we turned in: the next morning she was laid dead in her bed! She had suffered a heart attack.

Whereas this for me, her only close next of kin in this country arriving from 6,000 miles after so many years, I could but regard as a fortunate miracle arranged by our Creator for our mutual benefits. The first thing I had to do of course was to arrange her funeral and it was possible for her to share her husband's grave at St. Endellion churchyard close to the north Cornwall coast. It is a rare coincidence that the care of this very personal grave is in the hands of a Tristan born lady Rosalie Moncaster, who lives within 10 miles of the church. She kindly places flowers on their grave from time to time.

Reflecting back I think occasionally of my Great Aunt Amy Miller's beautiful home, Crosslands, outside Barrow-in-Furness not far from Furness Abbey; she had hoped to host my parents wedding in 1911 to be the wedding of the year.

Unexpectedly, my father was sent up to Scotland to inspect a warship's gun mounting when he was hospitalised for some reason near the River Clyde. The complete story is not known but only the main details. For some reason my mother and father decided to marry in Greenock Infirmary on 27 February 1911 and Aunt Amy was thus deprived of hosting their wedding in Barrow. She was so infuriated that she cast a spell on mother stating that if they ever had children may they never witness a wedding!

My sister Joan was the first to marry. She worked as a land girl in WWII and a Canadian officer whisked her off to Canada where they married in the absence of my parents. My second sister Stella followed her to Canada and she was pursued by a garage technician from England, they also married in Canada and again mother missed the wedding. Stella had worked in the R.A.F. in the war and then later in a garage in Sussex.

Pat the third sister qualified as a State Registered Nurse and followed me out to South Africa where she married a Rhodesian, so mother missed the third wedding.

As for me, I was the last to marry at 36, which I did in Cape Town Anglican Cathedral five weeks after meeting my wife on board the passenger ship *Stirling Castle* on a return voyage from Southampton to Cape Town in February 1949. A shipboard romance you will say – yes, but it was not premeditated and completely unplanned – but my mother was not able to attend the fourth wedding! The spell? I wonder.

But Great Aunt Amy's legacy had a very positive effect on us all. For me it lasted the whole of my life and into my 90s – not the size of the legacy but that it enabled me to buy that first class ticket in 1937 when I emigrated to South Africa and ended up in Tristan da Cunha, an interest for life!

~~~~

When the Tristan islanders were evacuated to England for their safety after the 1961 volcanic eruption, an expedition of vulcanologists was organised by Dr Ian Gass of Leeds University to examine the volcano and its effects. The Royal Society supported the project and I was appointed as Deputy Leader when they arrived in Cape Town en route for the island. We spent 6 weeks there, the vulcanologists studying the safety aspects vis-à-vis the islanders and I continued the weather reports.

A message arrived from the Cape that my naval reserve rank had been promoted to Lieutenant Commander, which to me was most gratifying. We were no longer R.N.V.R. but South African Naval Reserve officers. The hope I had expressed that by joining I might be able to visit some of my favourite islands

The Tristan Thatched Cottage – Home of Arthur and Martha Rogers.
My bedroom for several visits was the window on the left. (*photo ABC*)

during my time at sea certainly transpired: during the following years I made four extra visits to my friends on Tristan da Cunha, two visits to the uninhabited ice-bound Norwegian Bouvet Island in latitude 54° south, one visit to Marion Island in the South Indian Ocean, of the group known as the Prince Edward Islands, to establish a South African weather station; and one remarkable visit to the Great Ice Barrier of Antarctica where South Africa was taking over the operation of an abandoned Norwegian Antarctic Scientific Base.

～～～

In 1946 after the declaration of peace in Europe, Air Force meteorologist personnel who had joined up for service in South Africa were given the option of joining the civil service as meteorologists or reverting back to their pre-war employment. Still being single, I decided to transfer to the South African Weather Bureau as a technician on their staff. The first actual assignment I was given was to visit Tristan da Cunha to take over the weather reporting station from the Royal Navy on South Africa's behalf. It was an amazing project for me, for this was the occasion of my third visit to the island when I would be able to see all my old friends again.

Two radio technicians, Hawkins and Bennets, the Rev and Mrs A E Handley and I were the only expatriates on the island. He was sent down from England to act not only as Anglican clergyman, but to serve as 'Jack of all trades' to represent the local community for a two-year commitment. After we had settled in for a year or so, in 1948 I received a confidential radio message from South Africa which I had to answer personally. Fortunately, I could, in those days read the Morse code: it started "Prime Minister (Field Marshal J C Smuts) requests you to lead an expedition to establish a new weather-reporting station at an undisclosed venue." I had to answer then and there: again as I had no family commitments I replied in my basic Morse code "I will accept". I was able to take six Tristan Islanders with me as helpers and together with two technicians we sailed in *H.M.S.A.S. Good Hope* under Commander H E Fougsteadt from Tristan on 11 January 1948.

We arrived in the Cape six days later. We had only five days to prepare. We discovered on our departure from the Cape that we were bound for Marion Island in the South Indian Ocean. This was the larger of the two islands known on some charts as the Prince Edward Islands. Various naval and merchant ships had become involved in this exercise. The Islands, underlined in red on some charts had been regarded as British and were handed over to South African sovereignty in part recognition for services given during the War. These events are described in greater detail in my book *"Tristan da Cunha and the Roaring Forties"*. Marion Island was in Latitude 47° South and well in the Roaring Forty west wind belt!

In 1948 with the aid of the Tristan Islanders we had with us, I surveyed about half the island, as this had never been done before – only sketched from the sea. We had to abandon the station to a relief staff after a mid-winter storm in August of that year which damaged our stores. The ship sent to relieve us was the *H.M.S.A.S. Bloemfontein* under the command of Lt-Commander H.H. Biermann O.B.E. who later became Admiral, Head of the S.A. Navy.

The six Tristan men who had supported us during the nine months were glad to return to their homes before Christmas 1948. I was well treated by the South African government and given a long period of leave to visit my mother in England.

～～～

Other Royal Naval ships in which I spent some sea-time on interesting voyages were: H.M. ships: *Milford* (1938); *Magpie* (1955); *Burghead Bay* (1958); and *Protector* (1964).

The South African ships were *H.M.S.A.S. Transvaal* (1946), *Natal* (1947), *Good Hope* (1948) and *Bloemfontein* (1948), on which occasion she was under the command of Lieutenant-Commander H. H. Biermann O.B.E., later to head the newly formed S.A. Navy. The ship on this voyage was sent to replace us with relief personnel and stores which were damaged by a storm at the weather station .established on Marion Island in the South Indian Ocean.

An Extended
'Thomas Cook's Tour'

One of the more interesting jobs I had as a meteorologist was in the 1940's during the period towards the end of hostilities. It was to visit many scattered outlying weather-reporting stations throughout the south and west of Southern Africa. By virtue of my qualifications as an engineer I ranked as a petty officer and given the title of Sergeant Major in the Air Force. I visited very many places I would not have seen under normal circumstances of life; indeed I also met very interesting people.

Firstly a word or two about my work: it was to visit 'lay-observers' as they were called who were people in different parts of the country like farmers, school teachers, post office officials or even gaolers who were weather enthusiasts and offered to send by telephone or telegraph, at certain standard times every day, weather details like wind direction, barometer reading, temperature, clouds, rain, all details having to be written down in international standard figure code form. These details were required every day by telegraph at Headquarters in Pretoria in order to enable the compilation of weather forecasts. For this work the observers were paid usually on a three monthly or quarterly basis. My job as an inspector was to visit these observers, to check their instruments, encourage them to record their readings accurately and to bolster up general good relationships.

I went around the country mainly by rail and because the main test instrument I carried with me was a barometer, i.e. a delicate glass tube filled with mercury in a box about a metre long which required very special care, I was normally booked into a railway compartment called a coupé which I occupied singularly. I also sometimes travelled in a government car or could even order local taxis if there was no other means available. I was supplied with codebooks, cloud charts and record books, and when establishing a new observer I had to carry a level or theodolite to measure the height of the proposed mercurial barometer above mean sea level.

My visits depended so much on the work that had to be done and lasted sometimes from three or four days to two or three weeks and I had to stay at military camps where these were available, otherwise in local hotels. I visited lighthouses on the coast from South West Africa on the Atlantic side of the country to the South East bordering on the Indian Ocean, in addition to many towns in the interior on the rail link. I met so many interesting people that to me my work was a great joy and I likened it to an extensive 'Cook's Tour'.

Of particular interest was the mouth of the River Orange where it enters the Atlantic Ocean and forms the southern boundary between Namibia and Namaqualand, which was also on my visiting list. I had to test a barometer in a lighthouse at a small coastal village called Port Nolloth. This time I got the cooperation of a Norwegian costal shipping firm I knew called Thesens, so I got a free passage in the 250-ton vessel *Dalness*. We left Cape Town docks around 4.30pm on 17 August 1944 bound for Port Nolloth in a heavy southwesterly swell. Next morning we sighted a 100-ton coaster *William Holland* flying the distress signal. They were suffering from crankshaft and steering problems. We took them immediately in tow into a bay called St Helena where we anchored and spent a bumpy night. Next morning after getting rid of our disabled vessel into responsible hands, we proceeded north, arriving two days later at the isolated Port Nolloth where I was required to check the lighthouse barometer. This small village was close to the alluvial diamond bearing area strictly protected by police, as it was out of bounds for the general public, development being licensed to the firm that advertised that diamonds are a girl's best friend!

Five days later I caught the post-bus to Okiep, one of the most interesting places I visited in that area, where I had at least a fortnight's work ahead. Here I

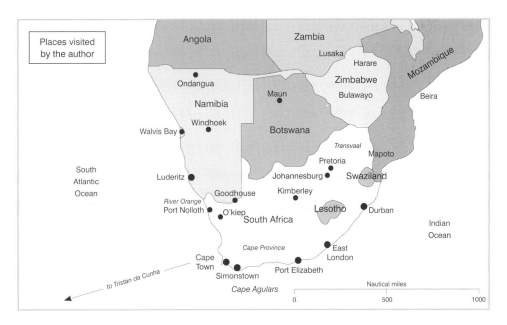

arranged to transfer the observing of weather to a new enthusiast, and the person selected in advance happened to be the 20-year-old daughter of an immigrant settler who was a person of mixed race and of unquestionable ability. I found her very suitable for the work she had to do i.e. the coding and despatching of daily weather reports. She was also favoured by the local postmistress who was of Afrikaans descent so I did not question the political implications, which could have derailed the project!

However I had in addition to normal work, met the local clergyman and his wife, Rev William and Doris Gregorowski, whose parish was that of Anglican Church in Okiep. They were to become great friends of mine, and of my wife when I eventually married, for the rest of their lives and were a great help to me while in their area, allowing me to work in their home. I boarded at the local hotel. There were several small towns in the vicinity including a couple of copper mines and hence, in those days, immigrants from Cornwall, my old county in England where my parents eventually ended their days. It was a bit like coming home to befriend these 'Cousin Jacks', as they were called in the gold mine regions of South Africa. They entertained me in Okiep and included Cornish pasties in their menus to make me feel at home.

The Gregorowskis, I discovered were descendants of German missionaries who had immigrated to South Africa in the early 1800's, one of the most famous of whom was Reinhold, born in 1856. He studied law at Cape Town University and Gray's Inn, London and from 1892 to 1896 was Advocate General of the Orange Free State. In 1896 he became a judge of the Zuid-Afrikaansche Republiek and conducted the trial of the Jameson Raiders for high treason, found them guilty and sentenced them to death, subsequently commuted to life imprisonment by President Kruger.

Because William and Doris Gregorowski had heard me talk so enthusiastically about Tristan that, when William was made an Archdeacon in the diocese of Cape Town under whose influence the Island fell, he made a brief sea voyage to the parish of St Mary on Tristan da Cunha on behalf of the Archbishop of Cape Town who was unable to visit this outpost due to more demanding engagements.

While on the subject of the William Gregorowski family who had three sons and one daughter, two of their sons followed their father's profession and became ordained priests; Christopher the elder of the two ended his profession as Bishop of Table Bay, Cape Town, in which diocese the parish of St Mary's church of Tristan fell. In 2003 when 15 parishioners needed confirmation, Bishop Christopher and his wife Margaret had a fascinating voyage from Cape Town to Tristan to confirm the candidates waiting on that isolated outpost.

They were entertained not only by the local priest and residents, but also by the Administrator and other officials. They regarded it as a wonderful experience coming towards the end of his professional life. He came to my home in Wadhurst in the July of 2005 with his sister Catherine (Cait) who was my godchild. She was born in 1949 and sadly died in London later that same year of their visit to me in 2005. Her memorial service was held at St Martin-in-the-Fields, Trafalgar Square on 25 July 2005.

To return to my business in Okeip, I had several dorps (villages) on my list – places like Pofadder, Springbok and Nababeep most of which I had to reach by postal lorry, sometimes even sitting on oil drums! An interesting observer I had to visit while in the area was the German Karl Weidner, a relic from the Great War days after which the German colony of South West Africa was then controlled from South Africa. I had to remove the instruments at Goodhouse, the name of the citrus fruit farm which Mr Weidner owned, from the north side of the river Orange to the south bank where his best fruit trees were located. The thermometers had to be changed from Fahrenheit to Celsius, which was now internationally recognised.

My headquarters staff in Pretoria had warned me they could not guarantee what sort of reception I would receive, as he was a 'bit of a character'. I had therefore been warned.

I took the post bus to travel to Goodhouse and was not greeted by him on arrival but by an employee. Seeing me in Air Force uniform no official introduction was forthcoming. However when he heard I could speak German, by the next day he had gradually 'thawed out' and I was lucky to receive a smile. When I presented him with the envelope containing his quarterly cheque for his weather records, he politely handed it back to me saying, 'I don't need your money! Go and hand it back to your Field-Marshall and tell him to go buy himself a sugar candy with it.' The person to whom he was referring was of course Field-Marshall J. C. Smuts, Prime Minister of the country and head of the Army Navy and Air Forces fighting for the Allied cause against the common enemy.

I reported this incident to headquarters in Pretoria on my return and with a chuckle from the Colonel-in-Charge they said I fared lightly! Their file on Goodhouse probably records similar, or even worse, rebuffs or cynicisms. I later heard that Karl Weidner had produced several newspaper articles relating South Africa's good or bad weather cycles with records from the Antarctic to which he had had access.

From Pretoria, I was then despatched to South West Africa, now Namibia, where I spent a couple of months at weather reporting stations including lighthouses at both Lüderitz and Walvis Bay on the coast, and inland stations Windhoek (the capital), Grootfontein and the fascinating native territory of Ovamboland close to the Angola border. In this area were Ovambos and Hereros, whose women folk were still dressed in the fashions of the Victorian era, in long dresses, long sleeves and spectacular headgear introduced by missionaries of a previous age. I longed to get a good photograph of one but was too embarrassed to break the ice! There were very few roads in this area and one had to cross the famous Etosha Pan, a huge lakeland area flooded in the summer by rains but dry and barren in winter where lions roamed in search of water and prey. We got stuck for some hours by grass seeds blocking our radiator causing the water to boil. We avoided the necessity to have to walk for the police for help at the old German fort of Namatoni as the engine cooled to normal and eventually we were able to proceed on our way.

During the period in 1946 when I was waiting to be demobilised, I was posted to Maun, in the land-locked country, which in those days was called Bechuanaland, now called Botswana. Important weather observations were still required from the centre of that area and staff at the weather head office in Pretoria were becoming redundant with less activity with the advent of peace. I was pleased with this transfer to Maun. I took my portable typewriter and the diaries and notes I had written between 1942 and 1943 on the 'Invasion of Tristan' during the war. I spent the evenings typing what eventually became the manuscript for another book not published until 2004, 60 years later, when I was in the 92nd year of my life!

Maun was indeed a small village in those days; it had if I remember rightly little more than a pub, a general store and a post office-cum-radio station situated in a 'rondavel' which basically was a round mud hut. The area was an important centre for the recruitment of Africans who were required to work in the South African Goldmines but I believe it is now the very different independent country of Botswana.

The people of that country have been described in recent years in the novels written by Alexander McCall Smith many of which I have read with nostalgic pleasure. The countryside was flat, level and swampy. Travel from South Africa was only accessible by rail to Francis Town and then by lorry over primitive countryside to the village itself.

It was more lonely than Tristan da Cunha.

Joyce Burch

My own marriage cannot be neglected, as it was not without its romantic and literally dramatic connections. Apart from the lady I met in Pretoria, who was beyond my reach, I had never had in my twenties a real girlfriend and by the time I was 36 I was getting worried.

In 1948 I went over to England to see my mother and although I was still single, I renewed the acquaintance of a family I had known in Barrow in the 1914-18 war days. One of the two sisters was already betrothed and after a brief encounter with the younger sister Joyce Marion Thompson, with a minimum of 'build up' I proposed marriage just before I sailed in the *Stirling Castle* on my voyage back to South Africa. I made a last minute impromptu telephone proposal and received the blatant rebuff – "No thank you. I would want to be properly courted before committing myself at such short notice!" was her answer.

Nevertheless, I boarded the ship in Southampton and set sail for the Cape. This time I was travelling tourist class at the cheapest rate possible. However, on board I met the head girl of Johannesburg (Witwatersrand) University who introduced me to her friend, a certain Joyce Burch, who at this same time was also returning to South Africa after visiting her parents, who had settled in England. Joyce Burch and I soon became close friends as her parents had been in India as had mine. In fact she was born in Bombay in 1913 where her father had been the manager of the Bombay Gas Works.

During the voyage I was confined

The Burch family, c1917
(*back l to r*) Betty, Dick, Ronnie (*sitting*) Joyce
Dick was a fighter pilot in the Royal Marines, Ronnie was in a Commander in the Royal Navy lost in command of a submarine. Betty taught HM The Queen and Princess Margarite dancing lessons during WWII.

to my cabin for much of the time with a temperature; but in spite of that Joyce was periodically able to break down the boredom by visiting me in my otherwise isolation.

Upon arrival in Cape Town we arranged to meet for tea on the attractive stoep (veranda) of the famous Mount Nelson Hotel, where I was tempted to propose marriage and to my surprise was accepted. As an afterthought, but a few weeks later, I wondered whether the subconscious had been working in my mind, because within the last month the two girls to whom I had proposed marriage had both born the same two names 'Joyce Marion'! However it is perfectly true that I did not even know that my fiancée's second name was also Marion until after my proposal!

Anyway, we were both 36 and decided we were responsible for our own actions. In fact within 5 weeks of our meeting on board, we were married on 2 April 1949 in Cape Town Anglican Cathedral by the Precentor, John Aubrey, who much to my gratification was a recently retired Royal Naval Chaplain.

We lived in Cape Town and I was able to introduce my wife to the Stannards as they passed through the city on a sea voyage to the Far East. They sojourned on the very night she played the lead, Judith, in Noel Coward's play *Hay Fever* performed at the University's Little Theatre. It was with pride I sat with them to witness her professionalism. They were old friends from Barrow.

To complete the story, Joyce was a full-time lecturer on the staff of Cape Town University, in the Speech and Drama Department. She was a well-known local actress, play producer and frequent broadcaster on Cape Town radio. I became known for many years as 'Joyce Burch's husband'!

Looking back I would say that it was a happy marriage in spite of the fact that we had completely different interests – which were as different as chalk is from cheese. I knew nothing about drama and she was not greatly interested in Tristan da Cunha.

When I went on pension in 1976 we had to come to a decision as to where we wanted to end our days. We started our lives as British citizens and by this time we possessed dual nationality so the choice was ours. We felt, however, we needed a change. Although we were mutually interested in local politics and would have liked to play our part to improve the situation we felt unable to do so.

There was another reason pulling us back to Britain. To make any political progress in South Africa it helped to be fully bilingual in two languages, Afrikaans and English and although as a civil servant I had a basic knowledge of the former (indeed I had passed what in those days was the matriculation in both languages) I was far from bilingual and it was too late to advance on that. Joyce on her part had been a lecturer in English at the most famous Afrikaans University of Stellenbosch that had produced several fully bilingual prime ministers. She was advised not to expend energy on learning Afrikaans otherwise her students might fail in their attempts to learn English. She certainly could not learn another language at her age. Thus the die was cast and we returned to England.

I for my part had additional interests in southern Africa in that I had life-long friends living in the Tristan da Cunha islands only 1,500

Joyce Marion Burch (Crawford)

sea miles from Cape Town, in the middle of the South Atlantic Ocean. In those days not many books had been published about this place and I was hankering after a visit to England where institutions existed, like the Royal Geographical Society, the National Maritime Museum and the British Library, where I hoped I could extract information to make up enough material to write a good book about the area.

In the end, I persuaded Joyce to retire to England for the later years of our lives, using as bait the selection of an abode in the proximity of London as a carrot to overcome her reservations. Here she would be close to one of the world's prime theatrical venues, enough to tempt any thespian. It worked!

We were lucky in 1977 to acquire a semi-detached house on the outskirts of Wadhurst, East Sussex, which we purchased from Mr John Bush, a retired petroleum geologist. We named our new home *Rosebank* which was also the name of the suburb in Cape Town in which we had lived for over 25 years.

I wrote my book, *Tristan da Cunha and the Roaring Forties* (published in 1982), and Joyce visited London's theatres. Much of our subsequent lives have been recorded earlier. As well as the display of beautiful roses in front, it had a small vegetable garden at the back for which I was responsible; so as soon as the raspberries, redcurrants and blackcurrants ripened, I set about my annual winemaking campaign! I had local friends who also bottled their own brews out of the proliferation of wild fruits like blackberries, sloes and elderberries. Joyce enjoyed being within easy reach of London and, in her later years, became greatly interested in developing a rose garden in which she planted over 100 mostly different species.

We both had family connections within East Sussex, where we settled, she near to her half-sister Miss Betty Vacani who during the World War II period had taught dancing to the Royal Princesses Elizabeth and Margaret in their formative years.

During our lifetime Joyce had been a good wife, had made clothes for me and even attended a tailoring course to create a jacket out of material we bought in the Hebrides. I took carpentry courses at our local Uplands Community College and made one or two items of furniture for our home.

Marilyn and Martin at Rosebank, South Africa (*photo Beau Rowlands, 2005*)

Martin Tristan Crawford, our elder son, was born on 24 January 1950 and married shortly before we left for England in 1976. Martin took over our old home in Cape Town where he was already working for a large assurance organisation.

They have two daughters and two sons. They both continue, not only my old connections with the Tristan islanders, but carry on some of the relationships I made with them. He and his wife, Marilyn, have great interest in the South Atlantic Islands of St Helena and Tristan da Cunha. From time to time they not only visit Tristan da Cunha, but also St Helena Island. They often host islanders when they visit Cape Town for medical reasons or while on holiday, transporting them to see various interesting locations.

Our second son Jamie has given me one grandson and four granddaughters. He has inherited his mother's interests and is Head of Drama at the West Kent College in Tonbridge, Kent. He lives with me in Wadhurst, East Sussex where he keeps an eye on my activities while writing my memoirs.

It was not long before I was recruited for light duties as sidesman and church councillor of the attractive church of St John the Baptist in the next village of Tidebrook. My Christian faith had been greatly intensified by my two great friends, Arthur and Martha Rogers, in whose simple home I had stayed for nigh on a total of four years when I was working on Tristan da Cunha. They were very devout Christians, not theologians by any stretch of the imagination, and in that way similar to my own thinking, for I have never studied theology. However, I had learnt enough in my life to have great faith.

Looking back with gratification I realised how certain events in my life had fitted together like a jigsaw. I hope my memoirs convey the fact that both my wife and I had happy and fulfilling lives in South Africa, each with our own respective interests, she in drama and me in meteorology.

Sadly, Joyce passed away just six months before our Golden Jubilee in October 1998.

A last thought: listening to 8:10 early morning service on Radio 4 on Sunday 27 November 2005, I learnt that the following Sunday, 4 December 2005, the 8:10 service would be broadcast from St George's Cathedral, Cape Town, with ex-Archbishop Desmond Tutu taking part. This was the self-same church in which I had been married on 2 April 1949, so it was with nostalgic reverence that I enjoyed listening in, not only to the service from a church I knew so well, but to hear the world-famous Archbishop Tutu broadcasting in his world-wide celebrational manner!

Productions in which Joyce was involved

Year	Production	Theatre
1943	*The Barretts of Wimpole Street* (Elizabeth)	Little Theatre
1944-1946	Productions of *Tobias & The Angel, Ghosts* and *Martine*	Little Theatre
1947	*A Woman of No Importance* (Lady Hunstanley)	Little Theatre
1947-1949	Radio Plays with Philip Wade (from BBC)	Little Theatre
1949	Production of *Our Town*	Little Theatre
1949	*Claudia* (Claudia)	Brian Brooke Theatre
1949	*The Beaux Stratagem* (Mrs. Sullen)	Little Theatre
1950	*The Ball at the Castle* (Produced by Gwen Ffrancon-Davies)	
1951	Produced *A Phoenix Too Frequent* (with Nigel Hawthorne)	Little Theatre
1953	*My Three Angels* (Emilte) with Joss Ackland	B. B. Theatre
1957	*A Country Wife* (Lady Fidget) with Leon Gluckman	Little Theatre
1959	*Under Milk Wood*	Little Theatre
1959	Produced *The Importance of Being Earnest*	Little Theatre
1960	*Lear* (Goneril)	Little Theatre
1964	*Romeo & Juliet*, (The Nurse) (Produced by Norman Marshall)	Little Theatre
1967	*Billy Liar* (Grandmother)	Little Theatre
1968-1970	Various Productions, Little Theatre & Cape Performing Arts Board	
1971	*A Winter's Tale* (Paulina) (Produced by Leslie French)	Open Air Theatre
1972	*Hedda Cabler* (Miss Tessnen)	Capab Theatre
1975	*Hay Fever* (Judith)	Little Theatre
1937-1977	Radio work throughout this period, including *The Living Room* with Emlyn Williams, *Romeo & Juliet* with Marie Hey, *Julius Caesar* with Bernard Brown and *One Eye Wild* produced by the author, Louis McNiece	

The late Nigel Hawthorne, famous British actor in the TV series, *Yes, Minister*, was one of Joyce's drama students at Cape Town University in the 1940s.

Our nine grandchildren

Shirley 24-10-75

Debbie 22-9-77

Lindsay 17-10-79

Bryant 8-8-80

Bronwyn 14-9-82

Murray 5-2-89

Briony 8-11-91

Jessica 1-5-95

Rhiannon 27-12-96

Whaling Taboo!

For a period after World War II, Britain, Norway, Holland, Japan and other countries carried out whaling operations, perfectly legitimately, as meat was required by hungry nations and the oil for the manufacture of margarine and other by-products was also an essential commodity on the market. In the 19th Century Tristan da Cunha was dependent to a large extent on American whaling fleets which operated in their waters in the southern summer seasons. Today this is a subject which is largely taboo and constrained by conservation and other restrictions.

The Royal Navy at their base in Simonstown issued daily weather forecasts for the waters around southern Africa, a vital service for shipping as well as for whaling operations in distant seas.

It was difficult to get whalers to co-operate by supplying the forecasters with weather reports on which to base their prognoses as whalers, like all fishermen,

Postcard sent from Tristan da Cunha by Captain Albert Veldkamp on 7 April 1993 painted by him (signed AJV) on the occasion of the visit of RMS St Helena and his wife Nini.

did not want to divulge their positions especially when they were in areas of abundant catches. The Navy arranged secret position code figures to add to their true positions to disguise them from competitors who might be eavesdropping on their radio broadcasts. Upon receipt the forecasters would subtract the code figures applied to the ship's position to enable the true one to be disclosed. The Dutch whale factory ship *Willem Barendsz* was a special co-operator as that company used Cape Town docks, on its voyage to and from Holland and the Antarctic waters, to top up their supplies. I got to know her navigating officer, the second mate, Mr Albert Veldkamp every time they called at the Cape. He became a great friend, as their ships officers were a very good weather reporting crew. I used to take him to the airport to show him how their reports were used to forecast the weather. He also visited my home.

When I returned to England on pension in 1977 I visited him in his home in the Netherlands where he had a wonderful collection of whalebone scrimshaw (decorated sperm whale's teeth) second to none, of great worth these days.

He had never visited Tristan da Cunha in his annual whaling operations and on retirement with the rank of captain, he joined our Tristan da Cunha Association and with wife Nini they joined a cruise ship, which visited the Island one summer season and sent me his painting of Tristan Island that accompanies these memoirs.

I learnt a lot about the history of whaling in the years I was working as a marine meteorologist and even made a visit to Thor Dahl's head office in Sandefjord, Norway where I met the managing director, Mr Lars Christensen who had sponsored our 1937 Norwegian Expedition.

An event that took place during World War II was that the Russians captured a German whaling fleet in some Baltic port and in 1946 launched into whaling operations in the South Atlantic. Because whaling operations were unknown to them they hired a well-known Norwegian whaling captain to keep them in the straight and narrow paths of whaling operations. They renamed their captured factory ship *Slava*. They called at Tristan da Cunha on their way south where I was stationed at the time. Captain Solianik and some of his officers came ashore and I captured a record of their visit on my 16mm movie camera. I recorded Solianik signing a large picture of Stalin, which he presented to Rev. Handley as a souvenir of their visit! At a later date they called at Cape Town for stores when I was working in the docks and they invited me and my wife to lunch on board with their agents and other official guests. The Norwegian captain was no longer with them so I guessed he had returned to his home on an earlier occasion.

Eventually the Navy handed over the sea area forecasting duties they had undertaken to the civilian authorities and standardisation was arranged throughout the world by the World Meteorological Organisation in Geneva.

(*Above*) Wandering Albatross taken on Marion Island in the South Indian Ocean on the occasion of establishing a new weather station after the war in 1948. The albatross was not returning to her nest after fishing, as the photo suggests – I had turfed her off to see if her egg was hatching. (*photo A.B.C.*)

Chick of Yellow-nosed Albatross, above Burntwood, Tristan da Cunha

Post-War Memories

Once back in harness in South Africa I was given wonderful consignments of work by our department in the Cape Town and Simon's Town areas.

The Royal Navy gradually pulled out of the area at the end of hostilities. They had provided the shipping weather bulletins which in peacetime reverted to the civilian pundits at the Weather Bureau Headquarters in Pretoria. I, as the so-called expert in maritime affairs in the south of the country, was the obvious person to undertake duties proposed by the World Meteorological Organisation (W.M.O) in Geneva. They recommended its members to appoint officials in important ports to allocate Port Meteorological Officers to contact ships to report weather by radio to the appropriate countries as they sailed around the world. I was the man to do this work for South Africa and I was most grateful for the full confidence they placed in me. It was a job I loved, dealing with shipping, working with codes, forecasts, communications (radio) etc. It involved representation as an 'expert' delegate for many international conferences in Geneva, Switzerland and several other countries involved in codes. This was a great honour for me, especially as South Africa's politics in those days was regarded by some with suspicion. However, delegates to scientific meetings were advised to neglect political matters at their conferences.

I visited Geneva seven times to take part in working groups during the last ten years of my employment; and I am not a little proud to say that I took part in sorting out the final recommended English wording of the upper strengths of the famous Beaufort Wind Scale, which (if I recollect correctly) were:

Force 8: Gale,   Force 9: Severe Gale;   Force 10: Storm;
Force 11: Violent Storm;   Force 12: Hurricane.

There were usually ten to twenty delegates present at these meetings, and our recommendations were submitted to higher authorities, like the 4-yearly meetings of the Commission for Maritime Meteorology (C.M.M.), No.1 of which I gather took place in Geneva or the U.K. in 1952, I first entered the sequence of meetings in 1956, which was C.M.M.II, held in Hamburg, Germany. I then attended the next 4 International meetings, C.M.M.III (Holland), C.M.M.IV (Switzerland), C.M.M.V, U.S.A. and finally C.M.M.VI, in Tokyo, Japan. All these visits lasted

Royal Navy Weather Forecasting Course M.21 held at H.M.S. Harrier, 1956 (*A.B.C. back row, left*)

for at least 2 working weeks, so delegates had the opportunity of benefiting from a couple of weekends for local tourism, where desirable. When in the U.S.A. I was enabled to spend a weekend in Canada where I had a reunion with two of my sisters, Joan and Stella whom I had not seen since 1937 – 31 years ago. I also visited the Niagara Falls, a great event.

On my visit to Tokyo, Japan to take part in C.M.M.VI, we had an extra week before the conference, at which our working group was required to display special instruments we had been working on. Between 1956 and 1974 I was involved in the development of instruments to be used from a moving ship at sea like the sea surface temperature thermometers. I was expected to explain the special bucket I had designed for this. So I had extra time, and travelled in the famous Bullet Train, visited the lower slopes of Mount Fuji and collected a pearl from a coastal port where they opened an oyster for a pearl which I bought as a present for my wife on my return to South Africa.

My three-week visit to Tokyo, Japan in 1972 was not without its romantic incident! I had been bidden to attend a technical conference to demonstrate a display of instruments on which I had been working for the first week. This was followed by the usual fortnight of our four-yearly longer C.M.M. (VI) Conference. Of course we could relax at the weekends between the two meetings and apart from my visit to the lower slopes of Mount Fuji, I made a trip in the famous Bullet Train at its maximum speed. The name of the train I learnt from a fellow passenger was the Kintetsu Limited Express and I was on my way to visit a small cultivated pearl farm to buy my wife a souvenir pearl ring from an oyster which I saw opened!

Japanese people are never backward in promoting their personalities, especially if they have a foreigner sitting next to them on whom they could practice their English. I was the victim and Michiyo Matsunaga, an attractive young lady in her late teens was the passenger. She adopted me then and there for the purpose of practising her linguistic skills. I told her, as the beautiful countryside flashed past outside that when my wife and I had got married we bought a Noritaki Japanese dinner service to celebrate our wedding and that it was still in perfect condition. It was then that she introduced me to her friend and neighbour who had remained silent because she could not speak English who turned out to be an employee of the factory that manufactured that famous Japanese china! That fact actually strengthened our newly formed relationship although after I left the train we never met again. But by our brief encounter I had inherited Michiyo as a permanent correspondent for several years to come. My status in her letters was promoted from 'uncle' to 'grandfather'! She sent me pictures of subjects like Mount Fuji, the very famous wave with Fuji in the distance, her examination results and a photograph of her wearing traditional Japanese Kimono Costume, which they wear on special occasions. We no longer correspond since my retirement in 1976.

Weather forecasts are issued all over the world these days and no aeroplane lifts off the ground without a weather forecast, which consists of surface and upper winds, temperatures, visibility and clouds for the whole flight or voyage. For this to be understood by peoples of different nationalities and languages, international codes have been devised by the W.M.O. in Geneva.

For example, if one wanted to forecast or report that the wind is coming from the north, in international code

The Great Wave – a woodblock reproduction of *Off Kanagawa* is one of the famous *36 views of Mount Fuji* series by Katsushika Hokusai (1760-1849).

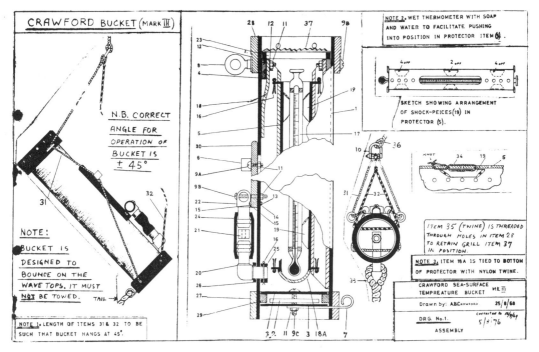

CRAWFORD BUCKET (MARK III)

N.B. CORRECT ANGLE FOR OPERATION OF BUCKET IS ± 45°

NOTE: BUCKET IS DESIGNED TO BOUNCE ON THE WAVE TOPS. IT MUST NOT BE TOWED. TAIL

NOTE 1. LENGTH OF ITEMS 31 & 32 TO BE SUCH THAT BUCKET HANGS AT 45°.

NOTE 2. WET THERMOMETER WITH SOAP AND WATER TO FACILITATE PUSHING INTO POSITION IN PROTECTOR ITEM (5).

SKETCH SHOWING ARRANGEMENT OF SHOCK-PEICES (19) IN PROTECTOR (5).

ITEM 35 (TWINE) IS THREADED THROUGH HOLES IN ITEM 28 TO RETAIN GRILL ITEM 37 IN POSITION.

NOTE 3. ITEM 18A IS TIED TO BOTTOM OF PROTECTOR WITH NYLON TWINE.

CRAWFORD SEA-SURFACE TEMPREATURE BUCKET MK III
Drawn by: ABCrawford 25/8/68
DRG. No.1. ASSEMBLY 5/8/76

SEA-SURFACE TEMPERATURE BUCKET / SEE-OPPERVLAKTE TEMPERATUURMETER

The 'Crawford' sea-surface temperature measuring bucket was invented, manufactured and tested over a period of a year or two and was demonstrated in England, the United States and Japan. The prototytpe bucket was manufactured, by the firm Zeal, in England, with a plastic body and made of PVC.
(*Temperatures these days are still measured using sea buckets, but also by satellite and other means*).

(*above*) Some of my drawings for the sea-bucket mark III.

(*below*) The sea-bucket in operation. Fixed in a sling it bounced across the waves. Its size can be gauged by the hand of the operator. The accompanying 10-page instruction booklet was written in English and Afrikaans.

(*facing page*) Charts showing sea-temperatures measured using the sea-bucket during 1968. Such charts could be used for fishing operations and also sometimes for forecasting fog, especially over cold water. The charts were analysed with temperatures received by radio from ships at sea over ten-day periods and issued by post for use by interested organisations. This service was initiated by the Port Meteorological Office.

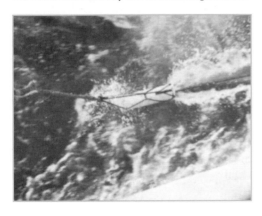

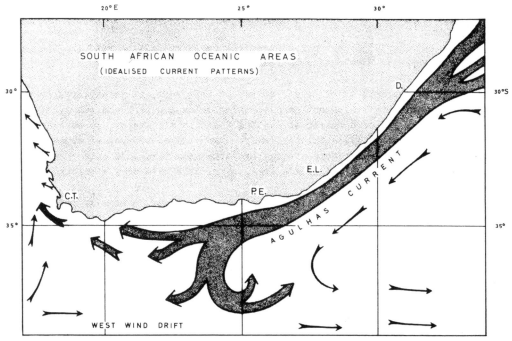

FIG. 1   THE SPREADING OF THE AGULHAS CURRENT
(By Nils Bang, Oceanography Dept., U.C.T. (C.S.I.R.), 1968)

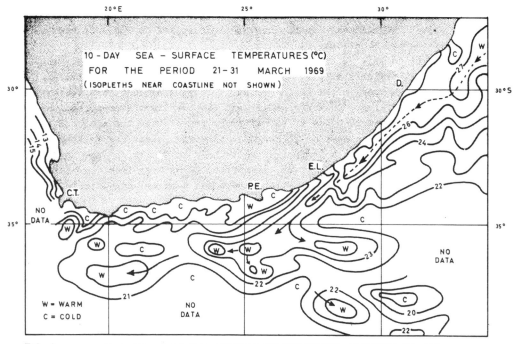

FIG. 2.   ISOTHERMS FOR SEA-SURFACE TEMPERATURES ADJACENT TO THE
SOUTH AFRICAN COAST, SHOWING AXIS OF MAXIMUM TEMPERATURES
(By A.B. Crawford, Maritime Weather Office, Youngsfield, Cape Town)

The five principal delegates at the CMM Conference in Japan, 1972
(*l to r*) K T Mcleod (Canada), K Terada (Japan), S L Tierney (Ireland), J M Dury (Belgium), A B Crawford (South Africa)

the figure used is 36, no matter in what language you intend. This represents 360° on the compass scale so, whatever language one uses, these two figures in a certain position in a code form represent north. It was of great interest and a great honour for me that I was selected by my superiors in Pretoria to represent South Africa on the Commission for Maritime Meteorology in Geneva.

When the 5th session of the C.M.M. planned to meet on 19 August 1968 I was sent over to Kingston, Rhode Island in the USA to attend the conference. I was in fact proposed as Vice-President of the Commission and had to fly to Washington to visit the South African Embassy for authority from Pretoria to accept the nomination should I be elected. In the event I lost the ballot by four votes which was not too bad amongst about 50 members! For me this was a significant outcome especially as the country I represented was regarded by some not with great political favour.

At the Commission for Maritime Meteorological (CMM) conference in Utrecht, 1960, as South African delegate.

My office in Cape Town was situated in dockland at *S.A.S. Unitie* the naval reserve base. In the course of my daily work I was completely free, and must have visited something like 800 to 900 ships a year of various nationalities; visits depended on their voyage routes. The second mate, the navigating officer, was usually my direct contact for negotiation and I will never forget the occasion when I was served by a second mate an intended gin and tonic out of a bottle which contained photographic developing fluid by mistake! The developer had been stored in an empty gin bottle. When he withdrew the toxic dose with apologies and replaced it with the correct ingredients I accepted his hospitality in the right spirit!

The work in the office became so important that we had to have a teleprinter installed so we had a record of the radio messages the ships transmitted whilst in our area. I introduced a prize scheme for the ships which sent us their reports. We awarded framed pictures provided by the Publicity Department consisting of local beauty spots. The pictures contained small plaques attached on which the ships name was engraved. These were welcome gifts of decoration on board a ship at sea, miles from land. I required an extra member of staff to man the office while I was absent visiting ships. In the early days of this new appointment I had an old retired Royal Navy Officer, Commander Hawke, who in his earlier days had been King's Harbour Master (K.H.M.) of Simon's Town dockyard. He was an attractive character to have as a companion in an otherwise lonely office; he had been a manager of a local cinema and had owned a restaurant, extraordinary occupations for a retired naval officer. Being a reserve naval officer myself we had much in common.

I usually had to go to sea for my annual training for a week or two from time to time so it was good to be able to have a presence in the office while I was absent. This meant I could often select a destination of my choice. Twice I visited Bouvet Island, a Norwegian owned but abandoned ice-covered island in latitude 53° South close to Antarctic waters.

On several occasions I went to Tristan da Cunha when either a Royal Naval or a South African ship visited the island.

~~~

During the decades starting from the end of World War II, I took part in several sea-going expeditions from the Cape of Good Hope in both British and South African ships, some of which ventures were motivated by the International Geographical Year (I.G.Y.). The main period of this project lasted for just over a year both in the northern and southern hemispheres, when countries extended their scientific investigations into areas unknown or even unoccupied. As a marine meteorologist working for the South African Weather Bureau I was involved in visits to islands like Tristan da Cunha, Gough and the Norwegian Bouvet Island in the far south of the Atlantic.

In December 1959 I made the most interesting voyage of my life. It was my luck to reach the Great Ice Barrier of Antarctica where we relieved a Norwegian International Geophysical Year (I.G.Y.) expedition team of scientists who, for economic reasons, were abandoning their base in favour of a team of South Africans who, for the sake of continuity, operate that area of Queen Maud Land still to this day in 2005.

We travelled in a small 500-ton Norwegian sealer *Polarbjørn* (*Polar bear*) and no sooner had we entered the pack ice when we got stuck fast for over a week and were unable to move. Then, after celebrating in the New Year of 1960, a trace of smoke was observed on the horizon and were unexpectedly rescued by the 5,000 ton Argentinian icebreaker, the *General San Martin*. We had not sighted a single vessel at sea in the fortnight after our departure from Cape Town! This ship was on her annual trip bound for their scientific base *Belgrano* in Antarctica with their annual stores and relief personnel. They freed us from our imprisonment in the pack ice, by breaking a channel so that we could sail away. We were soon rescued from our predicament.

The occasion was a godsend for me, as a I had been suffering from bad toothache for ten days and the icebreaker had a fully-equipped dental surgery on board. The two ships pulled up alongside each other, I climbed aboard and

(*left*) The 5,000 ton icebreaker *General San Martin* which arrived unexpectedly and rescued us from after being blocked for a week in pack ice. They had a fully equipped dental surgery on board and extracted my aching tooth. (*photo: ABC*)

(*right*) The 500 ton Norwegian sealer *Polarbjørn* (*Polar Bear*) tied up to unload stores and personnel on the Great Ice Barrier of Antarctica. (*photo: ABC*)

in no time at all my offending molar was extracted and jettisoned to Davy Jones'
Locker beneath the pack ice. We then continued our voyage to the Norwegian
base in Queen Maude Land, delivered our stores and scientists and embarked
the Norwegians for their repatriation via Cape Town back to Norway.

~~~~

At the end of 1954 a team of British scientists organized an expedition mainly
from Cambridge University to visit Gough Island which had only been manned by
sealers and whalers in its past history. Once again, when this base was abandoned
at the end of their work, the weather observations had proved so valuable to
shipping in the area around Africa that continuity was maintained by Britain
handing over the weather reporting facilities (but not the sovereignty) to be
maintained by South Africa, for which they faithfully maintain to this day.

South African scientists now occupy weather stations not only in the Antarctic
and Gough Island but on Marion, south east of the country in the Prince Edward
Islands group as well. All these bases are serviced annually by the Research ship
S.A. Agulhas, which includes Tristan da Cunha when she visits Gough. My last
visit to Tristan was in the *Agulhas* in 1984 – the cuisine was first class!

While on service in the port meteorological office throughout my days I worked
on designs for improving the measurement of sea surface water temperature
instruments including thermometers and electrical thermisters. The firm Zeal
of London helped with this research but now sadly no longer exists. Later our
office used to issue 10 day sea surface temperature charts of the east as well as
the west coasts of the country; this information was useful not only for fishing
operations but also for forecasting fog. The temperatures enabled operators to
locate the movement of the warm Mozambique and Agulhas currents on the
east coast and the upwelling of the cold waters on the west coast. In my office
I had also invented an automatic simple form of coder to convert basic plain
language weather observations into international code but I have not been left
with any descriptions of this and I expect all these ancient instruments have been
updated by modern technology like satellites 30 or 40 years on!

~~~~

If my memoirs are read by a meteorologist, he or she will appreciate this
comment: having learnt my lifelong weather in the southern hemisphere I
learnt that the wind in all lows and cyclones in that half of the globe rotate in
a clockwise direction, whereas in the northern hemisphere the winds rotate in
the opposite way round! Winds that rotate around a high-pressure system turn
in just the opposite directions, which in my old age became far too complicated
for me to consider forecasting weather for my friends in my retirement.

I have often been asked by people who realised I worked as a weatherman, what are the secrets in forecasting the weather, and why are the forecasts so often wrong? I usually replied that when an accurate count is made after the event, the forecasts are proved to be 80-90% correct. One so often remembers the odd occasion when they went wrong; meteorology is not an exact science.

International Conferences Attended

Year	Date	Name of Conference	Place	Details
1956	16/10-1/11	**C.M.M. II** (Commission for Maritime Meteorology)	Hamburg, Germany	"Crawford" Ships
1960	16-31/8	**C.M.M. III**	Utrecht, Holland	Demonstrated Weather Coder
1963	4-6/12	Weather advice for fishing operations	Geneva, Switzerland	Dr Terada
1964	23/11-8/12	**C.M.M. IV**	Geneva	Gave slide lecture
1965	1/10	To DFMALAN Rubber Bucket	Geneva	
1967	26/9-4/10	W/G Data Needs and Codes	Geneva	Crawford Bucket (gave lecture)
1967		To Youngsfield	Cape Town	Hydrographer
1968	19-31/8	**C.M.M. V**	Rhode Island, USA	Visited sisters in Canada
1968		Bucket		
1969	16-27/6	w/g Data Needs and Codes	Geneva	Bathyscape Affairs
1969		H.M.S. Dundas - Thermistor	UK	Tested instruments
1970	25-30/5	w/g Network at Sea	Geneva	(Tournier) Thermistor hose
1972	2-7/10	Technical conference on the Means & Acquisition & Communication of Ocean Data	Tokyo, Japan	Demonstrated instruments
1972	9-21/10	**C.M.M. VI**	Tokyo	Gave lecture
1972	4-8/12	w/g Codes	Geneva	
1973		w/g Codes	Geneva	

w/g = working group

Persona Non Grata?

I have been encouraged to include this chapter in my memoirs as it might ultimately result in the answer to the above question! I realize I might no longer be around if the answer does not come to light soon, but it's a good true story which merits recording nevertheless.

The world was amazed in 1961 when the supposedly dormant extinct volcano on Tristan da Cunha burst into activity. This occurred close to the village of Edinburgh; in fact the nearest house to the lava, that of Dennis and Ada Green, was burnt to the ground when a red-hot bomb landed on the thatched roof and set it alight.

The Administrator Peter Wheeler wisely had to evacuate the entire population to the United Kingdon for their personal safety. The Islanders were grateful for the measures taken on their behalf. They were well treated and cared for by the government and local organisations in England, but they were used to their independent lifestyle on Tristan and were not so happy in the clutches of the 'civilisation' into which they had been introduced.

The volcanic crater (*right*) with the village of Edinburgh on the left, with the sea in the background. Taken in 1962 on the Royal Society Expedition. (*photo ABC*)

I was in South Africa at the time working as a civil servant and had a few years earlier been made Honorary Welfare Officer for the Island in Cape Town. This was after the death of Mr Percy Snell, who had devoted many years of his life to the welfare of the people.

Early in 1962 most radio reports emanating from ships crossing the South Atlantic Ocean in the vicinity of Tristan indicated that the volcano had calmed down and no longer appeared to be a threat to the local area. These reports created great interest in the United Kingdom where the evacuees were waiting but longing to return home. Professional volcanologists were planning to visit the island to study at close quarters the effects it had had on the immediate environment. A group of experts under the leadership of Dr Ian Gass of Leeds University managed to get sponsorship and funds from the Royal Society in London. They formed a small expedition who flew to Cape Town where they foregathered to spend a couple of months on Tristan for the main purpose of ascertaining what effects the volcano had had and as a possible consequence whether the place would be safe for future re-occupation.

I was invited to join the party as weatherman and so accompanied them for the visit. In January 1962 we were kindly conveyed to the island in the South African naval frigate *S.A.S. Transvaal* and after our work there, returned back to Simonstown on 20 March in the Royal Naval Antarctic Research Vessel *H.M.S. Protector*, which was conveniently returning from the south to Simonstown at that time.

The outcome of the volcanologists report appeared to be that, in so far as human beings could predict volcanic activity, the Island was once more restored to its previous state of stability. They had noticed that a similar lava flow had taken place on the south of the island near Stony Beach about 400 years ago. It was possible therefore that another could break out in three or four hundred years time. Until scientists discover more reliable ways of predicting volcanoes and earthquakes, it is a case of *be not anxious for the morrow* (St Mat. 6, 34). I know the Islanders have experienced enough faith in the past to look after that eventuality themselves.

Meanwhile the Islanders were being looked after in sheltered accommodation not only by the Government in England but by organisations in the Southampton area and many had already acquired meaningful employment. However the sudden plunge into 'civilisation' was basically quite alien to them and they thought only of their homes and their property rights on the island, which they had been forced to abandon at such short notice.

People in England treated the evacuees with great respect and courtesy though residence in the civilised world was not the natural choice of a community that

A rather large cinder which broke away from the volcano and landed a few metres from the nearest house. One red-hot cinder landed on the thatched roof of the only house which was burnt to the ground. Staff Sergeant Bob Shaw, Royal Corps of Signals, (*left*) signaller of the 1962 Royal Society Expedition and Adam Swain one of the two Tristanian guides of the expedition (*right*).

had never even seen a horse and cart in their lives before. However, after a harsh winter in the UK and, to them, a complete lack of freedom they longed to return to their homeland..

It appeared that the Colonial Office, as it was then called, did not want to return them to what might be a dangerous environment, but hoped they would integrate into the British community with the advance of time. This evidently was just what the Islanders did not want and this upset them greatly. They realised their livestock of cattle, sheep, donkeys, etc., left on the island and their homes would all deteriorate rapidly the longer they stayed in England, which was indeed quite true.

As their ex-Honorary Welfare Officer in Cape Town, appointed in May 1955, I was perhaps one of the few who knew the Islanders and their local weather conditions so well, having lived on the island for several years in the past.

In desperation many families wrote to me requesting that as their now ex-welfare officer that I try to arrange their repatriation. They started writing from England to me in South Africa, family by family, pleading for me to attempt, if I could, to get them back to their island homes. It was not long before I was able to fill an empty shoebox with over 100 aerogrammes! It was obvious to me who knew them so well the frustration of their desperate situation. I realised I had

The three principal islanders of the 12 who volunteered to live on the island after the volcanic eruption. (*l to r, back row*) Thomas Glass, Lars Repetto, Joyce Crawford, Johnnie Repetto (brother of Willie the Chief) at my home in Cape Town. (*front row*) Jamie and Martin

to do something pretty dramatic on their behalf. I even suggested confidentially to Chief Islander Willie Repetto that if the Islanders became desperate, they could petition H.M The Queen to intercede on their behalf and suggested the form of letter they could despatch.

Although British by birth, I had acquired South African nationality by virtue of the work I did for that country, not only as a civil servant but also as a naval reserve officer. I did not want to blot my copybook so-to-speak in any way and did not want to be charged with interfering. However with a couple of aerogrammes stuffed into my pocket, I called on the British Ambassador Sir John Maud one morning in 1962 and gave him my story of support for the Islanders' case. As he was bound shortly for London on a routine visit, he promised to promote the Islanders' case in the right quarters.

By the same token, I called on the Royal Naval Commander-in-Chief, South Atlantic, Vice-Admiral Sir Nicholas Copeman, R.N. explaining with greatest respect, how it was only Islanders who could decide whether their homeland was fit for re-occupation and the urgency of the situation.

Rumour had it from the UK that the authorities were going to ask the Navy to estimate this by a shore visit. Only Islanders could do this effectively after witnessing weather cycles and beach landing conditions for several months of observations. Volcanologists even could not predict when, if ever, the island would erupt again but the authorities had their report.

Both gentlemen took sympathetic attitudes towards my reasoning which was indeed encouraging. In fact the British Admiral invited me to submit a plan which I considered a great opportunity and which I ultimately did with great pleasure.

It was one sleepless night followed by a second when I produced what turned out to be a winner. I kept closely in touch with Mr C. H. Gaggins of Cape Town who was Managing Director of the company that operated the crawfish processing factory on the island whose building had been completely inundated by the molten lava. Mr Gaggins had also lost his island workforce and of course wanted to renegotiate a new licence to fish in the area, which was important for his future planning. He made several visits from Cape Town to London during his negotiations and was a valuable confident of mine exchanging information on the progress of thought and attitudes prevalent in the UK.

Drastic measures were vital. The plan I conceived was to recruit 12 island volunteers to save up and buy their own tickets to Cape Town, that I considered the authorities could not stop, and I would get Mr Gaggins to take six men to live on the island and to clear up and to study local conditions, and he would have the other six to employ to help him reinstate his fishing operations. Fortunately he was fully supportive of the plan, which was named the Resettlement Survey Party. I followed it up by communication to Willie Repetto, the Chief Islander, which, of course, was greatly to their liking.

I have no idea what went on in London and no one ever communicated with me except my two Islander friends Arthur and Martha Rogers in whose home I had lived for several years in the past. Then one day, almost unexpectedly in August 1962 the Resettlement Survey Party arrived in Cape Town in the ship *Stirling Castle*, the ship that had taken them to England almost a year previously! The colonial office must have approved my plan, for they included Mr Gerry Stableford an agriculturalist to accompany the party as observer. He was known to the Islanders, having worked there previously. He was to submit a confidential report on his return. All went well both for the Islanders and the authorities, for by April 1963 an advance party of 51 island men and women returned to prepare their homes for the rest of the community. By 24th October the remaining 198 men, women and children left Britain with their goods and chattels and were conveyed direct in a specially chartered Danish ship (the suitably named *Bornholm*) landing in November 1963. Two years of civilisation had proved enough, but it had done a great deal of good to the Islanders educationally, and had brought them up-to-date.

In the meanwhile, I continued my work in Cape Town docks and on one occasion whilst walking past a vessel which was docked alongside and loading with stores for Tristan da Cunha I met an Administrator who attacked me with the remark "You went too far beyond the point of reason with the steps you took to get the people back to their Island!" I was so much taken aback by this remark that I was speechless and continued on my way without comment!

On another occasion, when I went to sea in a South African Antarctic Research vessel *R.S.A.* on a voyage of investigation to the Norwegian Bouvet Island, the captain related to me the incident when he arrived at Tristan da Cunha on a previous voyage to deliver passengers and stores. As soon as he dropped anchor, the Administrator came on board and asked him the following question:

"Is Crawford on board?"

"No," replied Captain McNish, "Why?"

"That's good," replied the Administrator "because I would not have allowed him to land! He is persona non grata as far as the Colonial Office is concerned."

I was glad to receive this early warning because this same ship in which I was travelling, was destined to call at Tristan da Cunha after our work on Bouvet Island was complete. I did not want to suffer the indignity of not being allowed to land at Tristan after all the work I had done there in the past twenty years or so.

It so happened that I had, without previously knowing it, a miraculous solution to my personal predicament. Captain M. S. Ollifant R.N., in *H.M.S. Protector* the Antarctic research vessel, was en route from the south to the Royal Naval Base Simonstown in South Africa, when he was directed by the authorities to call at Bouvet Island to help us with our research work. The ship had a helicopter on board so that was a great asset.

To overcome my difficulty I asked Captain Ollifant if he could give me a lift back to South Africa 'in order to keep a dental appointment' a request to which he readily agreed. He even sent his helicopter to assist my transfer from *R.S.A.* to his ship so I avoided the indignity of not being 'allowed to land at Tristan!' On board *H.M.S. Protector* were old friends of mine Martin Holdgate, Peter Baker and Commander Wynne-Edwards, all welcome shipmates.

During the year that preceded the volcano eruption i.e. in 1960, I was delighted to meet in Cape Town the American clergyman Rev. Robert Mize who had come from Kansas City on a year's sabbatical leave presumably to study at first hand conditions in Southern Africa. Rev. Mize was an ordained priest in the Episcopalian Church, the equivalent of our Anglican Church in the Province of South Africa. Soon after his arrival Rev. Mize was offered a passage in *H.M.S Puma*, a 2,500 ton British warship that was about to leave Simonstown for a visit to Tristan da Cunha. He was requested to study the conditions of the local inhabitants and on his return submit a report to the Archbishop of Cape Town as the welfare of the island's church fell within his diocese. I met Robert Mize on his return when he submitted his five-page detailed report. He had much appreciated his visit. In fact he was so much enamoured by the local population that he wrote to the authorities offering his services should a vacancy arise for the living of the island parish! Ironically enough, the island itself provided the dramatic answer to his offer, for it burst into volcanic activity in October 1961, and the whole population was evacuated to England for their safety.

A few months after his return, Robert Mize was consecrated Bishop of Damaraland which was the ecclesiastical area centred at Windhoek, South West Africa. Robert and I had a great deal in common with our mutual love and understanding of the Tristan da Cunha population.

Some years earlier I had been invited by the church in the Cape of Good Hope to serve on the managing committee of the Missions to Seafarers, a charity they operated in Cape Town docks for the benefit of ships' crews of any nationality who needed help in any way whilst in Cape Town harbour. It was in these docks I too had my offices as a meteorologist. Additionally I also supported the local church ashore, which in its early days was the beautifully thatched church of St. Thomas, Rondebosch, a suburb of Cape Town.

And so it was that on one day in 1963, after most of the islanders had been repatriated, back to their island homes, Robert Mize whispered in my ear that the Archbishop of Cape Town, the late Rt. Rev. Joost de Blank, had proposed to honour me for my work with the 'Medal of the Order of Simon of Cyrene', as the mainly Anglican community on Tristan da Cunha was within the Diocese of Table Bay, Cape Town. The award is presented to a limited number of workers in the Province. I greatly appreciated the receipt of this, which in part mitigated for me in some measure for the lack of

Medal of the Order of Simon of Cyrene

understanding on the part I had played in the repatriating of the islanders back to their homes mentioned earlier in this chapter.

～～～

Under the circumstances I considered I took the right actions on behalf of the Islanders' predicament. I eventually destroyed my files so that at any future date the records would only be known by me.

The Islanders' rights were restored and their wishes achieved. They are now happy to be back in their homeland, which they have occupied since 1816 – nearly 190 years.

Visit to Tristan da Cunha in *HMS Magpie* in 1954 with the Gough Island Scientific Survey. I met my godchild islander, Martha Green (*centre*) with Joan King (née Rogers) now settled in England (*left*). The crawfish factory behind is now non-existent, having been completely covered by lava by the 1961 volcano.

13

The Versatile Potato

It was not only Norwegians amongst the Scandinavians who were interested in isolated islands. The well-known Swedish marine artist, Roland Svensson (1910-2003), who lived at Nacka, Stockholm and painted amongst his own country's islands but had, *inter alia*, visited lonely Foula, off the Shetland Isles, in 1954. His interest in Tristan da Cunha was aroused after he heard of the volcanic outburst in 1961, when the islanders had to be evacuated to Britain for their safety. He visited them not only in Britain, but when the government chartered the Danish ferry *Bornholm* to repatriate them back to Tristan in 1963, he joined the ship to accompany them. He admired the islander's stoicism and the islanders found him a good friend and respected him greatly. After several subsequent visits to the island, he eventually established the Roland Svensson-Enstrom Fund to give financial help at Christmas to the elderly folk who were too old to work. His special friend on Tristan was Lars Repetto, the former treasurer of the crawfishing processing factory who in those days administered the fund. Lars Repetto incidentally was born on 7 December 1937, the day on which we (the Norwegian Scientific Expedition) arrived at Tristan da Cunha. He was named after the sponsor of the expedition Lars Christensen of Sandefjord, Norway. Lars is married to Trina Repetto, née Glass, the locally trained school teacher who retired in 2005 after over 40 years service in St Mary's school. They remain on my mailing list to this day.

Roland Svensson and I had several common interests, like for example we both on separate occasions helped the authorities the Crown Agents in the designing of sets of postage stamps for the Tristan da Cunha post office when it was eventually re-established. Roland, in his capacity as a superb marine painter with his exceptional artistry, and me, with my penchant for historical research who then recorded sketches on the backs of envelopes! But my connection goes back a little further to the days before money was introduced on the island in the 1940's.

During World War II when I was employed on Tristan da Cunha as a meteorologist in the South African Air Force, I had the idea of producing a weekly newsletter entitled *The Tristan Times* to convey to the local community not only news items concerning the local population, but also the progress of

Dr Roland Svensson at home, 1987, late of Storangen, Nacka, Sweden.
Roland was a marine artist and author and a friend of the Tristan da Cunha community.

the war in the northern hemisphere. I had anticipated this project before I sailed from Simonstown and was armed with a small duplicating machine, my portable Underwood typewriter, stencils and adequate stocks of foolscap paper. I recruited as my 'foreign correspondent' the Medical Officer-in-Charge of the station Surgeon-Commander Woolley to copy information from the BBC overseas bulletins of the progress of the War. Every Saturday night, as Editor I compiled and printed *The Tristan Times* in preparation for the following day.

We had two types of readers, islanders on one hand and Royal Naval sailors and we three airmen on the other. But there was no money on the island whatsoever as this was in the days before its introduction. However, the islanders used forms of bartering in general and the commodity most often used was the potato. They could use potatoes to pay for their weekly newsletters but the sailors could not grow potatoes, so it was decided to charge expatriates cigarettes! Generally speaking the price of *The Tristan Times* was based on 4 potatoes or 3 cigarettes a copy! Two island 10-year-old boys, Harold Green and Linsay Repetto, distributed newsletters after church on Sunday mornings with gunney bags in

The penny red with a local value of 4 potatoes.

which to collect the potatoes. The naval doctor, who had a wife and two children resident on board and hence had a household to care for, took the potatoes in return for the latest wartime news. I have no recollection of what happened to the weekly haul of cigarettes as I was not a dedicated smoker but I expect some of these ended up amongst island men.

I was repatriated to South Africa in 1943 and undertook various inspections of weather reporting stations as described elsewhere. In 1946 just after my demobilisation I was requested to take over the naval station on Tristan da Cunha on behalf of the South African government to whom it was loaned. To me this was just my cup of tea.

Realising that virtually the whole island would derive a considerable income from worldwide stamp collectors should postage stamps be introduced, I quickly designed a set of stamps before I returned. But the same problem arose with which we had been faced in wartime – there was still no money on Tristan da Cunha, and indeed no official post office at all. However expecting that matters would develop in the future, I designed a set of ten stamps from one ha'penny

My designs for 10 stamps in support of the petition for postage stamps for Tristan da Cunha. Local values were shown as potatoes.

Only the penny stamp was printed and is now sought after by collectors. Artwork by Jimmy Brown of Johannesburg.

76

to two shillings and sixpence, giving each stamp an equivalent value in potatoes, based on the fact that four potatoes would be worth one penny.

In 1946, on my return, a petition signed by all the island councillors and the Rev. Handley was submitted by return to the authorities in the 'outside world' suggesting the printing of postage stamps at some future date.

Twenty thousand of one 'stamp' (the one designated one penny, or local value 4 potatoes) were printed in Johannesburg not intended for postal purposes but as a 'sticker' to advertise the project.

Although twenty thousand of these stickers were printed I gave most of them away to the island families who I knew would be able to barter them for clothing etc. with passengers on passing cruise ships. But it is true to say that the 'stickers' achieved unexpected publicity and became much in demand by interested collectors. Indeed the 4 potato stamp acquired official status when it was inadvertently printed on an official miniature sheet to commemorate the centenary of the death of Sir Roland Hill, inventor of the penny postage. It was promulgated on behalf of the island by the Crown Agents for Tristan da Cunha in 1979.

My late friend Roland Svensson, I am glad to say, had no problems with his designs for stamps for Tristan da Cunha. He even supplied designs for St Helena amongst his lifetime achievements.

I started helping the Crown Agents with designs in 1980 for the commemoration of the 150th Anniversary of the Royal Geographical Society. I often wondered if I was the first person to design into a postage stamp, the 15p stamp, my own chart of Tristan Island, which I personally had surveyed in 1938. I then supplied designs for ten more different sets of stamps in the 1980's.

Ironically enough one day when I decided to give a so-called 'potato stamp' to Bronwyn, one of my grandchildren, who lived in our home, I found that I did not have one single potato stamp left. The situation was rectified by my friend Ron Burn of Bromley, an avid stamp collector, who kindly provided me with one, which I gratefully accepted and presented to her in a small frame.

That event however left me once more without a single potato stamp, when unexpectedly one day I mysteriously received a small parcel which arrived by post and contained a potato stamp in a silver frame from two members of our Association, donated by our vice-chairman Guy Marriott and our enthusiastic American member Mike Mueller with kind words engraved around the frame – a very welcome presentation indeed. Strange when I thought back on the day in 1946 when I had 20,000 'stamps' printed for the price of little more than £15 the lot!

Presenting Bronwyn, my granddaughter, with my last 1d potato stamp.

Presentation of the 1d potato stamp, mounted in a silver frame, kindly donated by Mike Mueller and Guy Marriott
(*l to r*) Mike Mueller, Liz Evans, me, Guy Marriott, Ron Burn

14

Life in My Nineties

I have often been asked what is the secret of reaching your nineties? This I could not easily answer but I could detail some facts that might have had a bearing on my status quo.

Towards the end of my school days, instead of having a secret puff of a cigarette behind a closed door, I managed to wait for the time when I could openly display a packet of cigarettes and offer one to a colleague as I had witnessed was the custom. But although I must admit I did smoke too, no one ever suggested I drew the smoke into my lungs. The thought never entered my head; and now, thank God, I never did. When I got married my wife was a smoker and it always perplexed me why in the evenings when she ran low on stocks, I should have to sally forth to the local shops to replenish her supplies. However I was thankful on the arrival of our second son when she suddenly took a disliking to the habit and we both gave it up forever. Who knows maybe our abandoning the habit in our forties might have been a factor contributing to longevity for she lived into her eighties.

Another factor towards long life might have been my tendency to avoid binge drinking. This control I can put down to the fact that, being a civil servant by profession, and having limited finances, I enjoyed the occasional beer or shandy but I did not distribute my limited assets in the local pub. Only once after a naval social celebration did I overstep the mark; this time on brandy which was relatively inexpensive in South Africa. I never did know how I managed to drive safely home and get myself into bed unobserved; but I remember I felt so awful on the following day, that I vowed I would never do that again!

When I eventually went on pension and returned to England with my wife, my gratuity from the South African Government covered the relatively modest 3-bedroom house in the country without the necessity of a mortgage. I was a churchgoer and after 4 years service as a sidesman was invited to be a warden which kept me slightly occupied though the lady with whom I shared the duty, Mrs Janet Hardy Smith, was a hard worker and an instructor in the charity Riding for the Disabled. She was the brain behind our partnership. I retired as a warden when I realised I was beginning to forget the names of some parishioners (due to advancing age). I discovered my colleague and I were both born in 1912, me early in August and she on the 28th of the same month, so we were almost 'twins'.

Mrs Janet Hardy Smith lived on her own in a cottage with helpers but at the age of 93 had to move to a care home in Tunbridge Wells. I was lucky enough to get the local district council to subsidise the conversion of my downstairs loo into a shower-cum-toilet, which they carried out with great professionalism and consideration, for which I am greatly thankful. I now sleep in what was originally our dining room and rely on meals-on-wheels, which are delivered, to my home four times a week.

Tina Lindfield, my home help and 'Jill of all trades' since 1992. A great help to me.

On Thursdays my home help, Tina Lindfield, arrives to do morning household chores. Tina cooks my lunch before she completes her work. Tina was employed as our home help when my wife was alive. I was glad to re-employ her as she was virtually a 'Jill-of-all-trades' and indeed 'mistress of all'. Not only is Tina a good general home help but also my barber to cut my hair, a painter to touch up or even paint a whole room, a seamstress to mend my clothes and darn my socks, occasionally a gardener to prune raspberries and a manicurist to cut my fingernails (I employ a chiropodist to cut my toenails).

She also acts as a taxi-driver for necessities like a visit to the bank or surgery in the village. My fortune in finding such an accomplished individual was indeed far beyond my worldly imagination.

~~~~

When we bought Rosebank we were lucky to inherit a plot of raspberries, red and black currants that our predecessor, John Bush, had maintained so well. My cousin Mollie Ellis of Battle provided netting protection to save our fruit from the birds. It was not long before I started to make my own wines as blackberries, elderberries and sloes added extra fruit to our products. The switch to real grape wine came in the 1980's when our daughter-in-law Ann-Marie visited Germany with a class of students. As a souvenir of her visit she brought me back a cutting of a wine-producing grape, which I planted, on the south facing wall of our kitchen, with ideal results.

After a couple of years and a good season I had turned my vine into real wine, the cutting producing over 8lbs of fruit each year. I had a cousin over 90 years of age, Marjorie Hopkins of Englefield Green, who also had a very successful vine on the south facing wall of her kitchen which produced 20lbs of grapes a season, for which she had no use in later life. My friend Miriam and I used to drive over to her, not only for a good lunch but to collect her crop of unwanted grapes to add to our output. Miriam too was an enthusiastic wine maker.

Eventually, due to arthritic fingers in both hands, I had to postpone my wine-making days to a Thursday, which was the day my home help Tina visited me every week, in time I converted her into a very willing vintner, in spite of the fact that she remained a strict teetotaller all her life! How lucky I am to have her for such important work.

~~~

At the age of 93 I was encouraged by my family and even distant friends and relatives to write my memoirs. I even employed Tina for three hours a week on Monday evenings to act as my secretary and prepare my manuscript for my typist. My arthritic fingers had inhibited my ability to communicate my manuscript direct to the typist. Everyone had recommended I use a computer but I had never used such an instrument in my life before, and only advanced from a portable to an electric typewriter. My arthritic fingers had but put a stop to modern technology and I had to go the hard way.

However I was immensely fortunate being able to stay in my own home, albeit a little lonely in the daytime, though somewhat consoled by the presence of two friendly cats which I found good company.

~~~

My younger son, Jamie, in my 90th year, came to share my home. He eventually provided me every day with my evening meals and most meals at weekends so I only required meals-on-wheels on limited days.

Within sight of my 93rd birthday, and with some assistance from Jamie, my son, and Tina, my home help, who supplemented the inadequacy of the currants from

Wadhurst Park, I made 2 gallons of blackcurrant wine to celebrate the occasion, though of course it will not have completed its maturity until later in the year.

The lay reader, David Payne, of our small church St. John the Baptist in Tidebrook in the next valley, is a close neighbour and friend and his wife Betty was allocated by the church to keep a special eye on me.

I have another special friend Miriam who lives but a few dwellings near to my home. She keeps me supplied with postage stamps and other necessities from the local village shops. I am a member of a retired man's club called Probus, which arranges seasonal lunches or suppers in neighbouring country hotels or restaurants. I take Miriam as my guest on these occasions but she does the driving for I surrendered my driving licence on my 90th birthday.

~~~~

In 1995, aged 83, I thought that my life must surely terminate on an ever-approaching day! I had collected by that time memoirs, archives of records, photographs, albums, books, stamps, etc. and considered it vital I should place them in some institution while I still had a state of mind which could be categorised as compos-mentis, for to pass them on unlisted might have resulted in chaos. I passed on stamp and cover collections to close relations, but I had been invited by the late Dr Brian Roberts, pundit of the Scott Polar Research Institute in Cambridge to pass on my personal archives to that institution on my demise. He had known of my travels in the southern hemisphere, which included visits to several islands as well as to Antarctica. I considered the invitation a great honour. The archives were to be stored for posterity and used for research purposes. This handover of archives took place in 1995 and my contribution comprised eleven box files the contents of which are all listed. I was proud of the fact that this collection was driven up to Cambridge by a Tristan da Cunha born lady, my friend Lorna Lavarello who was living in Eastbourne married to her first husband at that time. Lorna succeeded me as Chairman of the Tristan da Cunha Association and had been educated partly on the island and later in the UK. I knew her Tristan parents and grandparents long before she was born.

I was invited by Dr John Heap CMG, Director of the S.P.R.I. (Cambridge) to design an escutcheon to be placed inside the books and other gifts I had presented to the Institute and for them to supply the wording to be placed inside. I based the design on my old school motto, taken from Wellington School Somerset, which was *Nisi Dominus Frustra*, including the logo of the Tristan da Cunha Association which I had designed and drawn of an albatross with the island in the background.

My archives are now available for research at the Institute.

The Allan B. Crawford Gift

Papers and Records relating to

Tristan da Cunha

Gough and Marion Islands
and
Bouvetøya.

The escutcheon placed inside books and other gifts presented to The Scott Polar Research Institute, Cambridge.

A significant milestone took place on 31 December 2001 when my name was included in the New Year's Honours List for the award of the M.B.E. for my work on behalf of the community of Tristan da Cunha.

I was accompanied by my son, Jamie, my grandaughter, Bronwyn, and Dr Sally Burch, my late wife's niece of London University.

In presenting the award to me at Buckingham Palace on 19 March 2002, H.M. Queen Elizabeth expressed great interest in the welfare of the Tristan Islanders, an interest that has been maintained by the Royal Family since Queen Victoria's days.

One of the latest events in my 94th year was a luncheon in our local Commemoration Hall organised entirely by volunteers, to celebrate the retirement of our non-stipendiary cleric Revd. Rosalie Alford. She has served our local community's three parishes – Wadhurst, Stonegate and Tidebrook churches – for many years with much professionalism and is much loved by all 170 guests who attended the ceremony. She had previously specialised as a teacher in Greek and Latin. Fortunately for us she is remaining in our area and able to help should an emergency arise. I first met Rosalie at evening woodwork classes for adults over 20 years ago; she still attends these classes, a very active lady!

Alice Glass (née Swain) who was appointed, at the age of 21, in 1937 to be our domestic help. She was a lovely girl, singing sea-faring songs as she worked keeping our quarters spotless. In 2005 she is my oldest regular correspondent.
(*photo: Janice Hentley 2005*)

Investiture at Buckingham Palace, 19 March 2002 (*courtesy BCA Films*)

My guests at my Investiture
(*l to r*) Bronwyn (my grandaughter), me, Dr Sally Burch (my late wife's niece), Jamie (my younger son).

A Memorable Weekend

The most memorable weekend of my life involved eight people between the ages of 90 and 102 and was celebrated on Saturday 9th and Sunday 10th of April 2005.

The occasions involved were on Saturday the 9th, when the Annual General Meeting of the Tristan da Cunha Association, was held at the Fountain Court Hotel at Hythe, Southampton, and on the following day the celebration of the 90th birthday of a relation, Jo Cotton, formerly of Horsham. This was conveniently on our way home to the Tunbridge Wells area.

On 15 April 1987, eighteen years ago, a group of interested people, after witnessing the success of the Falkland Islands Association followed their example and formed the Tristan da Cunha Association.

Our inaugural meeting was held at the Royal Geographical Society in London and included not only people who had served on the island in war and peace time but doctors, clergy, teachers, scientists, ex-administrators as well as philatelists and others who had never visited the Islands but had some special interests in the area. We formed a committee, which included two or three Islanders who were resident in this country, one Lorna Lararello who succeeded me as chairmen. We held Annual General Meetings in various centres like Uttoxeter, Oxford, Cambridge and the New Forest near the residence of Peter Wheeler the administrator who had brought the Islanders to England after the 1961 volcanic eruption.

Michael Swales of Denstone College, Uttoxeter was a force majeure behind the project in that he offered his services as honorary secretary, treasurer and membership secretary, whereas I was appointed Chairman and first editor of our Newsletter, produced then in black and white unlike the superb colour editions produced today. Membership is open to people of various interests. An Annual General Meeting is held in springtime and normally copies of our newsletter are issued free to members twice every year.

And so on Saturday 9 April 2005 our Annual General Meeting was arranged to be held at 2pm at a hotel in Hythe near Southampton Water. My friend and dentist, Liz Evans, had agreed to drive me down to the area. She was already a life member of the Association and had driven me with a wheelchair to Cambridge

Allan Crawford (Life President), Michael Swales (2005 Chairman), Mrs Lorna Smith (previous chair)
at the 2005 Annual General Meeting of the Tristan da Cunha Association in Hythe, Southampton.

where we held our previous meeting. This time we were accompanied by her friend Sally McKenzie who is now a special friend of us both.

I heard a rumour that the oldest member of our Association who was about to celebrate his 100th birthday on Sunday 17 April hoped to be able to attend as well. He is Surgeon Commander Eric King-Turner, R.N. (retd.). He and I had sailed together as shipmates in 1955 aboard *H.M.S. Magpie* from Simonstown to Tristan in the days when the Royal Navy sent a ship from time to time to look to the welfare and good health of the Tristan people. Eric was the dentist on board.

It is interesting to note that *H.M.S. Magpie* was the ship captained by H.R.H. The Duke of Edinburgh many years ago when serving in the Royal Navy.

There are two more significant links between Dukes and Tristan da Cunha. In 1867 the second son of Queen Victoria, Prince Alfred, Duke of Edinburgh, called at Tristan on his round-the-world voyage of *H.M.S. Galatea*. He lunched ashore and the Islanders were so impressed with his presence that they gained his consent to name their village Edinburgh in his honour. Our present Duke of Edinburgh called at Tristan in the *R.Y. Britannia* in 1957 when he went ashore and laid the foundation stone of their new Prince Philip Hall.

Our Annual General Meeting took place as arranged with such success that it was deemed the best we had ever had! Over 100 members and guests filled

My two helpers, Liz Evans (my dentist) and Sally McKenzie.

the room, events were held throughout the day with the formal A.G.M. at 2pm followed by other activities in the evening.

Liz, Sally and I spent Friday and Saturday nights with Liz's mother, Mary Seward, who was in her 90th year. She lived only 10 miles away from Hythe, near Lymington, in her fascinating and beautiful home in the country.

As President and being in my 93rd year I was determined to make a special effort to attend this meeting as I thought it might be my last! It was wonderful to see so many old friends again, especially the Tristan Islanders. Ada Green, one of those present, was a Brownie who tried to teach me Semaphore in 1947 when I asked Mrs Handley, the school teacher, to lend me Brownies for this purpose. Mrs Handley, the wife of Rev. A. E. Handley, sadly died at the age of 97 within a month of the meeting.

Being both dentists I introduced Liz Evans to our 100-year-old Commander King-Turner with the result that they had a long conversation. We wondered, out of curiosity, what they were discussing at such length? Liz informed us that he was explaining how to repair broken dentures on an Island like Tristan if vital materials were not available. This could be achieved by melting down old 78 gramophone records on a stove to make a special tray and using beeswax to make an impression and a bite. The procedures needed lengthy explanations but it was all Greek to us!

Interested in weather reports from whaling ships in the days when they operated in the Southern Ocean, I had acquired a sperm whale's tooth that was given to me on board a factory-ship, which called at Cape Town docks. This I gave to Liz to supplement the Rhino's tooth she acquired in Zimbabwe many years ago. She used both enormous teeth to impress juvenile patients in the magic of dentistry. The sperm whale's tooth weighed 340 grams, 50 times heavier than a human molar.

On Sunday 10 April on our way home we were invited all three to attend a family celebration in the beautiful home of Stephen Cotton, Chailey Moat in East Sussex where his mother, Jo Cotton, was celebrating her 90th birthday. She was connected by marriage to my late wife. The celebrations included singing by trained choristers of several generations of Cottons who are a very musical family.

My two friends Liz and Sal proved to be great outgoing characters in the company of all whom they met and I was lucky they attended to all my needs so graciously. Sally is a superb photographer.

I regarded this past weekend to have been the most memorable of the whole of my life.

The National Oceanography Centre, Southampton

There were very special links I developed with Southampton, which began when I departed from that port in November 1937 on my adventurous voyage in the Union-Castle Mailship *Arundel Castle* for Cape Town in South Africa. This voyage was the first I made between the two ports for these were the days before regular air flights. My intention was to look for a job as a qualified engineer in the dominion of South Africa. I have detailed elsewhere the people I met on board that vessel and how, on our arrival in Cape Town my ultimate destination became Tristan da Cunha, a British Island in the middle of the South Atlantic Ocean and my meteorological work thereafter.

In an earlier submission of my manuscript for publication I had suggested that sea temperatures were probably recorded by radioactive means these days which raised doubts in my publisher's mind. He contacted the National Oceanography Centre in Southampton to verify my assertion and was put in contact with Dr Elizabeth Kent of the Centre's Ocean Circulation and Climate Division.

It transpired that Dr Kent had been preparing a series of papers and had referred extensively to my work on sea-surface temperature measuring instruments on which I had been working for the World Meteorological Organization in Geneva, Switzerland many years ago. She even had a copy of the drawings of my sea bucket pinned to her office wall. I learned that the subject of accurate water temperatures was still important throughout the world to be received from ships at sea while crossing oceans especially for monitoring global climate change, in which research Dr Kent was very much involved. Sea buckets are still in use alongside other methods, such as satellites, buoys and the water intake of some ships.

Dr Kent contacted me and visited me at home. It was a great pleasure to lunch together at the Best Beech Inn along the road. I showed her my buckets specially designed for measuring the data involved on a worldwide basis. She was also interested in the relevant files and literature involved. Arrangements were provisionally made to hand all this data and archives over to the National Oceanography Centre in Southampton.

I later approached Dr Pauline Simpson, Head of Information Services, custodian of the library and their archives to discover if they would be willing to accept a donation of some books, records, charts and laminated collages, which I had accumulated since 1995 when I donated my life's archives about my travels in the Antarctic waters to the Scott Polar Research Institute in Cambridge. I handed many of these records to the late John Heap who was director at the time, for he and his wife Peggy broke their journey from a visit to a colleague on the south coast, to lunch with us in Wadhurst. Eleven box files filled with additional archives I delivered personally to Cambridge later in the year. I was then in my 84th year and had not expected to add an additional 10 years to my life!

However there was a special reason why I had wanted to find a home for my further Tristan da Cunha archives in the Southampton area.

In 1961 the island burst unexpectedly into volcanic activity. Fearing that it could perhaps develop into a second Krakatoa, the 263 islanders were evacuated for their safety by Administrator Peter Wheeler to England. They were brought by sea from Tristan to Cape Town and thence by Union-Castle Line ship *Stirling Castle*, landing in Southampton.

The islanders were eventually housed as a group in the then abandoned R.A.F. base at Calshot at the end of Southampton Water and the Solent. The Tristan people spent two years in that area and they made many good friends in Hampshire. But the weather during their first winter was the worst for many years and the lifestyle in civilisation was completely alien to people who on the whole had never seen a brick building nor even a horse and cart in their lives before. Almost to a man, they just wanted to return to the home they loved. This was the goal that they ultimately achieved towards the end of 1963.

However, the island community had never forgotten the kind people of Hampshire, the Red Cross, the Mothers' Union and similar organisations who befriended

Other sea buckets in the National Oceanographic Centre's collection, Southampton (*photo © Barry Mann Photography*)

Allan explains the finer details of his sea bucket to Dr Elizabeth Kent in the library of the National Oceanographic Centre, Southampton. (*photo © Barry Mann Photography*)

Allan presenting his sea temperature measuring bucket to the National Oceanography Centre collection and archive. (*from left*) Dr Jeremy Grist, George Mann (*back*), David Berry, Pauline Simpson (Head of Information Services), Allan Crawford, Liz Evans, Dr Elizabeth Kent, John Zeal, Dr Margaret Yelland (*back*). (*photo © Barry Mann Photography*)

them while they were in the area. It became my ambition to try to find a home for the additional archives I had accumulated near at hand; that would be convenient not only for local people who would recollect the fascinating visitors who sojourned in their midst in 1962-1963, but also for islanders themselves who remained in England, or who have subsequently settled here, and for whom Cambridge S.P.R.I. is far to far away to visit.

Islanders have told me it was the hand of the Almighty that enabled them all to derive the benefits by visiting the United Kingdom, whereas without the volcano, few of the inhabitants would have been able to see the 'outside world' in a lifetime.

Crawford Point ~ To Be or Not To Be?

hat certainly was the question when completing my 1938 fair chart of Tristan da Cunha Island in Simonstown under the guidance of the Fleet Navigating Officer, Commander Tupper-Carey R.N., informed me that it was perfectly in order in those days for a surveyor working on virgin territory to place his own name on an unnamed promontory needing one. It constituted a record of historical value to be aware of the surveyor's name. I was not over enthusiastic to append my name to the geography of the island for I made a point of recording the islanders' own names for every single feature I identified and found no suitable feature for me! However, in order to satisfy the pilot, as the Naval Navigating Officer was called, I chose an insignificant area on the West side of Hottentot Gulch, which I labelled Crawford Point.

As far as I can recollect, that was the end of the story. During wartime only weather charts were part of my life, for I had joined the Meteorological Section of the South African Air Force as a technician. In peacetime, as a volunteer member of the RNVR (South African Division), I went to sea in both British and South African ships and on one occasion when I revisited my old wartime venue of Tristan da Cunha and was anchored off the island, I decided to call on board the small 624 ton crayfishing vessel *Tristania* which was also anchored in the offing. My intention was to make a friendly call on the Master, Captain Morris Scott, known locally as Scottie. He was a man who called a spade a spade and was not particular about his use of language.

As I stepped on board Scottie took me straight to his chart room, opened the door and showed me his latest navigation chart of the South Atlantic and started to give me hell for putting my name on the chart thereby replacing the popularly accepted name of Cave Point. This was news to me and it was already a fait accompli. It was against the whole policy of my surveying procedure to change accepted local nomenclature. I did not agree with the uncouth manner in which he introduced me to the subject but I did agree with his attitude towards the undesirability of changing place names which are already established. I felt he wasn't convinced when I told him it had been nothing to do with me!

Islands & Seamounts in the South Atlantic

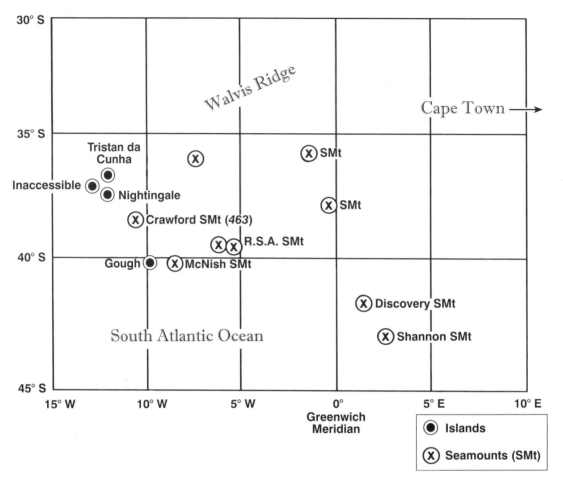

Sketch plan showing some sea mounts and islands in the South Atlantic between 30° and 45° latitude south of the equator and 15° west and 10° east of the Greenwich meridian. The positions shown are approximate.

Seamounts are upheavals which occur as the result of deep sea volcanoes which have not reached the surface of the sea. When they grow higher they form islands, such as Tristan da Cunha and Gough.

I had been so upset by the incident that when the voyage was over and I had returned to my office in Cape Town, I wrote to the Hydrographer in London and although I thanked him for the honour of putting my name so prominently on the chart, I pointed out that Cave Point was a well-known long-established local feature, and would he please reinstate the previous name as the change was already causing confusion? Thankfully this was done and charts were corrected accordingly. The future Admiralty chart No. 1769 stated in its heading *Tristan Island surveyed by A. B Crawford Esq. in 1937-8*. That was adequate acknowledgement for me.

With the benefit of hindsight I was able to conclude that when the chart had been updated during wartime the cartographer who was consigned to do the corrections, conscious of the insignificantly small headland I, as surveyor, had selected for my name, he with all the goodwill in the world had expunged my name from its original position and gave it a boost for better status elsewhere. Cave Point has been a landmark of great historical and cartographical importance, an area of great beauty, fur seals and penguin rookeries and the caves sheltering islanders when they needed to overnight when visiting cattle which graze in the vicinity and which are, or were in my day, all privately owned.

There was one quite unrelated development that took place after the acknowledged removal of my name from the Tristan chart. One workaday in the mid 1960's, the Professor of Oceanography of Cape Town University – whose name I have sadly forgotten – phoned me at my office in Cape Town Docks to enquire if I had any objection to the naming of an isolated seamount in the South Atlantic halfway between Tristan and Gough Islands after me?

"No," I replied, "but what have I done to deserve such an honour?"

"You leave that matter to us," was his short reply.

Of course I thanked him, but never thought more about it for several decades until when inspecting the contents of an abandoned file I rediscovered Crawford Seamount with the figure 463 beside it, with no indication whether this is the depth in metres, fathoms or feet.

Until, if ever, this seamount decides to erupt, to pop up and become solid land above the surface of the ocean, I will not bother to place it on the property market! I will just think of it dormant and contented below the surface waters so agitated in the "Roaring Forties" of those latitudes.

The Pieces of the Jigsaw

1912	Born 1st August, Conwy, North Wales (British).
1922–27	Craig Preparatory School, Windermere.
1927–30	Wellington School, Somerset.
1931–36	Engineering apprentice, Vickers Armstrong, Barrow. (Higher National Certificate in Mechanical Engineering).
1937–38	Member of Norwegian Scientific Expedition to TRISTAN DA CUNHA as Surveyor. (Admiralty Chart No. 1769 is still my survey).
1940	Joined Royal Geographical Society.
1941	Wrote book *I Went to Tristan* (Foreword: Admiral Sir A.E.R.G.R. Evans).
1941–45	War service in South African Air Force as Meteorologist.
1942-3	War service on Tristan da Cunha in charge of weather station.
1946	Awarded B.E.M. (Military Division for War Service).
1948	In charge of weather station, Marion Island.
1949	Married Joyce Burch, broadcaster and lecturer (2 sons).
1949	Awarded Cuthbert Peak Grant, Royal Geographical Society.
1950	Served as Port Meteorological Officer, Cape Town Docks, post recommended by World Meteorological Organization (Geneva).
1952	Joined R.N.V.R. (South Africa Division) as Meteorologist. Retired as Lieutenant-Commander.
1954–72	Attended international conferences as maritime meteorologist in U.K., Geneva, Holland, Germany, Japan and U.S.A.
1955	Appointed Honorary Welfare Officer for Tristan da Cunha in Cape Town by Colonial Secretary Mr. Lennox-Boyd.
1960	Invented Sea-surface Temperature Bucket, promoted by World Meteorological Organization.
1961	Visited Bouvet Island and Antarctica on meteorological matters.
1961–63	Initiated repatriation of Tristan da Cunha islanders on their request, after volcanic eruption on the island (1961).
1963	Awarded Order of Simon of Cyrene by Archbishop of Cape Town for services to Tristan islanders.
1976	Went on pension. Returned to Wadhurst, East Sussex, UK.
1980–	Visualized importance to U.K. of British Islands in the South Atlantic Ocean; joined Falkland Islands Association, St. Helena Link Committee and Friends of St. Helena Society.
1982	Wrote book *Tristan da Cunha and the Roaring Forties*. Foreword by H.R.H. The Duke of Edinburgh. Visited Tristan da Cunha for seventh time, this time with son and grandaughter.
1984 onwards	Designed 10 sets of commemorative postage stamps for Tristan da Cunha including special issue for the Royal Geographical Society's 150th Anniversary: *Flags*, *Shipwrecks* (13 series), *The Lost Lifeboat Centenary*, *Flightlessness*, etc. including 4 photographs to celebrate the End of World War II (50th Anniversary), to appear on 19 June, 1995. Formed the Tristan da Cunha (UK). First Chairman, and Editor of the Tristan da Cunha newsletter for the first 16 editions.
1992	Retired as Chairman and appointed the Tristan da Cunha Association's first President.
1980-1991	Eleven years as Churchwarden, Tidebrook Church in Wadhurst, East Sussex.
1995	Presented (upon request) 11 box files of my life's archives to the Scott Polar Research Institute, Cambridge University, for posterity.
1999	Published book Penguins, Potatoes & Postage Stamps, Anthony Nelson Publishers (now defunct)
2001	31 December: Awarded M.B.E. in New Year's Honours List.
2002	19 March: Presented with my M.B.E. by H.M. Queen at Buckingham Palace investiture.
2003	Made Life President of Tristan da Cunha Association, UK.
2004	Published book Tristan da Cunha: Wartime Invasion, George Mann Publications, Winchester.